D1648672

30-SECOND
SHAKESPEARE

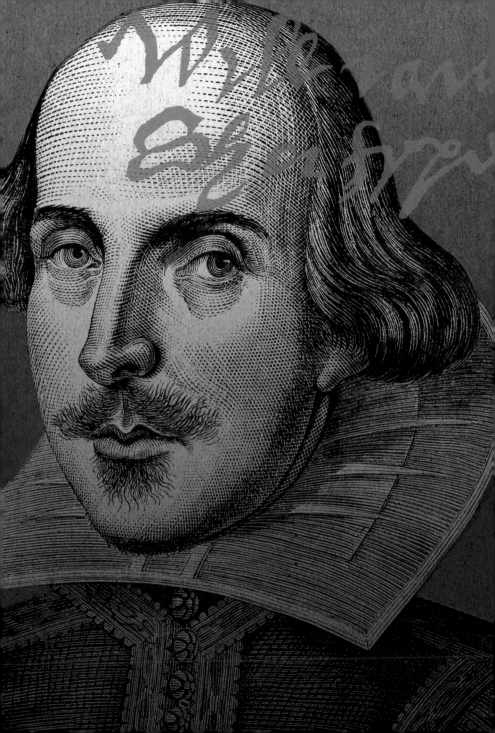

30-SECOND
SHAKESPEARE

THE 50 KEY ASPECTS OF HIS WORKS, LIFE & LEGACY,
EACH EXPLAINED IN HALF A MINUTE

Editor
Ros Barber

Foreword
Mark Rylance

Contributors
Ros Barber
Jessica Dyson
Andrew James Hartley
Margrethe Jolly
Claire van Kampen
Kirk Melnikoff
Lynn Robson
Lee Joseph Rooney
Earl Showerman
Robin Williams

Illustrations
Ivan Hissey

IVY PRESS

This edition published in the UK in 2018 by
Ivy Press
An imprint of The Quarto Group
The Old Brewery, 6 Blundell Street
London N7 9BH, United Kingdom
T (0)20 7700 6700 **F** (0)20 7700 8066
www.QuartoKnows.com

First published in hardback in 2015

© 2017 Quarto Publishing plc

All rights reserved. No part of
this book may be reproduced or
transmitted in any form or by any
means, electronic or mechanical,
including recording, or by any
information storage-and-retrieval
system, without written permission
from the copyright holder.

British Library Cataloguing-in-
Publication Data
A catalogue record for this
book is available from the
British Library

ISBN: 978-1-78240-515-3

This book was conceived, designed
and produced by
Ivy Press
58 West Street, Brighton BN1 2RA, UK

Creative Director **Peter Bridgewater**
Publisher **Susan Kelly**
Editorial Director **Tom Kitch**
Art Director **Michael Whitehead**
Senior Project Editor **Caroline Earle**
Commissioning Editor **Jacqui Sayers**
Designer **Ginny Zeal**
Illustrator **Ivan Hissey**
Picture Researcher **Katie Greenwood**
Glossaries Text **Ros Barber**

Printed in China

10 9 8 7 6 5 4 3

CONTENTS

FOREWORD
Mark Rylance

Thirty seconds? Speaking Shakespeare in 30 seconds I only get to 'Aye there's the rub' in the 'To be or not to be' soliloquy. But I am notoriously slow. 'To leave or not to leave. Get a bloody move on,' was a message I received backstage when I played Hamlet. I once heard two actors battle it out on the Globe stage to determine who could speak 'To be or not to be' the fastest. Mr Colin Hurley established himself that evening as the fastest Hamlet in history. I just texted him. 'I think it was about 32 seconds,' he texts back, 'any faster than that and you lose some of the poetry.'

The appreciation of speed is nothing new. Hermogenes (Greek Philosopher, 2nd century CE) praised Speed as one of the seven essential qualities of the perfect orator. Speed makes a speech seem lively and mobile, he wrote. I agree. Appropriate speed. Clarity, Grandeur, Beauty, Ethos, Verity and Decorum were the other essential ingredients of an eloquent speaker. Eloquence is defined in *The Oxford English Dictionary* as the action, practice or art of expressing thought with fluency, force and appropriateness so as to appeal to reason or move the feelings.

So what is the appropriate speed for enjoying Shakespeare? Thirty seconds? Fine with me. In 30 seconds I can say 'Hang there like fruit, my soul, till the tree die.' I could say it again and still have time to say 'We are such stuff as dreams are made on', or 'time hath my lord a wallet at his back'. That's enough for my reason and feelings for some time. And so, in the words of the character Speed (*Two Gentlemen of Verona*), I'll commend you, *30-second Shakespeare* book, to my master, William Shakespeare, and wish you good speed throughout the world.

INTRODUCTION
Ros Barber

More books have been written about Shakespeare than about any other writer or creative person. So what particular use is this one? The wide-ranging nature of the subject, compressed into a condensed format, might make it very useful indeed. We may come across Shakespeare at school, we may even study or see a play or two, but most of us are unlikely to go much further. After 400 years, Elizabethan English is more or less a foreign language and one to which few of us can naturally relate. Yet we also become aware that Shakespeare is everywhere in our culture; he and his works are constantly name-checked, and if we don't get the references, we are missing out. This book aims to make Shakespeare interesting and comprehensible by cutting out the waffle and boiling the subject down to its essence in order to explain what makes Shakespeare's poems and plays so uniquely important, interesting and durable.

The man-shaped hole

Most general-purpose books about Shakespeare focus on the man; most academic books focus on the works. But the man – or rather the historical record connected to the man – is so unsatisfactory that some people question whether he wrote the works at all. Bill Bryson described Shakespeare as 'the literary equivalent of an electron – forever there and not there', and historian Michael Wood described Shakespeare's biography as a 'man-shaped hole'. Shakespeare biographies are obliged to recycle the same unsatisfactory material, padding it out with conjecture and assumption. This general-purpose book, written by scholars, does away with conjecture, focusing instead on the central body of work that made Shakespeare a household name.

The Globe
Originally built in 1599, many of Shakespeare's plays were first performed at the Globe. The theatre was rebuilt in the 1990s, such is the Bard's enduring appeal.

THE·SHAKESPEARE·CLASSICS

The humanity-shaped whole
For what matters about Shakespeare is not the man, but the humanity found in his works. The whispered intimacy of his sonnets. The psychological insights of his plays. Tragedies that grab you by the collar, pull you into the darkness and stab you in the belly. Comedies that undress you and stand you in front of a full-length mirror to laugh at yourself. Histories carved into the flesh of your past by men who Shakespeare shows us were fully human, whether they were a tavern-keeper or a king. Though now touted as a god, Shakespeare was fully human. He understood the human condition better than most and expressed it better than any, in compressed and poetic truths that we have quoted so often they're now part of our language. What has made Shakespeare endure beyond any other writer is his gift for concisely revealing us to ourselves.

How this book works
The first chapter explores the **context** of the works – the society, influences and sources that shaped them – as well as the baseline of biography, exploring what we do and don't know about the writer and his writing. If we might know him through his **themes**, the second chapter looks at seven subjects to which the author repeatedly returned. Chapter three addresses some perhaps surprising aspects of his **knowledge** and four examines the essential **components** of Shakespeare's works. Chapter five looks at his **heroes and villains** and six unravels his interest in **magic and monsters**. Finally, we examine his **legacy**. Each entry is made up of the **30-second play** that delves into the subject, further distilled into a **3-second prompt**, with an additional **3-minute call** raising a question or focusing the spotlight on an interesting detail to explore further. Feature spreads in every chapter focus on a single play as an example of Shakespeare's genius.

The Weird Sisters
In Macbeth *and many other plays, Shakespeare explored all aspects of humanity – light and dark, good and evil.*

CONTEXT

anti-Stratfordians People who doubt that William Shakespeare of Stratford-upon-Avon wrote the plays and poems attributed to him.

blank verse Verse that is written in a regular meter (a fixed rhythmical pattern) but doesn't rhyme. Blank verse is usually written in lines of iambic pentameter, where the syllable pattern 'weak-STRONG' occurs five times per line. Blank verse is different from free verse, which has no rhyme or fixed rhythm.

Claudius The uncle of Hamlet who became king by pouring poison into his brother's ear and marrying his brother's wife (Hamlet's mother, Queen Gertrude).

commedia dell'arte A form of theatre that began in Italy in the 16th century and is characterized by stock characters of fixed social types. Best translated as 'comedy of craft', it entailed improvised performances based around certain scenarios, often around sex, jealousy, love and old age.

dramaturgy The theory and practice of dramatic composition. Distinct from playwriting and directing (though one person might do all three), it involves putting a story into a form that can be acted, incorporating all the elements of drama, with an awareness of a play's history and social context.

Elizabethan Pertaining to the reign of Elizabeth I of England (1558–1603). Those alive during her reign might be called Elizabethans and their practices, Elizabethan.

epigram A short, witty poem expressing a single thought or observation. Epigrams were particularly popular among the witty trainee lawyers of the Inns of Court in Elizabethan London.

epyllion A long narrative poem that has formal similarities (in theme, tone or style) with epic poetry, but is considerably shorter.

First Folio The *First Folio* is the term most often used to describe the first hardback edition of Shakespeare's collected plays, which was published seven years after his death in 1623. The actual title of the *First Folio* was *Mr. William Shakespeares Comedies, Histories & Tragedies*.

Hamlet Perhaps Shakespeare's most famous play, and the name of its leading character.

hanged, drawn and quartered A particularly gruesome Elizabethan punishment reserved for those found guilty of treason. Traitors were hanged by the neck until almost dead, disemboweled and emasculated while still alive, then beheaded and chopped into four quarters. These pieces were often put on public display.

Jacobean Pertaining to the reign of James I of England (1603–1625).

the King's Men The name of Shakespeare's theatre company after 1603, when King James VI of Scotland became King James I of England and subsequently their patron.

Nonconformism Not conforming to the practices and beliefs of the Church of England.

Ophelia Young, tragic heroine of Shakespeare's *Hamlet*.

patronage The means whereby a wealthy member of the nobility gave money or other forms of support to a writer or artist. Writers would often dedicate works to a wealthy Lord or Lady, hoping for financial support in return.

play-broker Someone who acts as the chief play-buyer for their acting company, and who might also sell these plays to a publisher.

revenge tragedy A tragedy in which the primary driver of the plot is a need for revenge.

satire A type of comedy that uses exaggeration, irony, and ridicule to expose and criticize the behavior of individuals. Usually topical and often used as a means of undermining those in power.

sonnet A poem (usually about love) of 14 lines with a fixed rhyme scheme and regular meter (pattern of rhythm) and a 'volta' (turning point), allowing it to, for example, both ask a question and answer it.

tragicomedy A play that is both tragic and comic.

THE LIFE & LEGEND

the 30-second play

Tradition holds that William

Shakespeare was born and died, with poetic appropriateness, on St George's Day, 23 April. This is possible, but not provable: he was baptized on 26 April, 1564 in Stratford-upon-Avon and buried there on 25 April, 1616. The third of eight offspring (five surviving), he married at 18 and fathered three children; his only son died aged 11. By late 1594 he was a shareholder of the Lord Chamberlain's Men (later the King's Men) and five years later he was a shareholder in the Globe Theatre. But beyond the texts, Shakespeare left posterity little by which to know him: no letters, no manuscripts, and a will whose most interesting feature is the fact that he bequeathed his wife Anne 'the second best bed'. Where history fails, myth fills the gap. Numerous stories abound of Shakespeare having to leave Stratford after poaching deer, or of holding horses outside a London theatre, or of being a schoolteacher in the country, or of having 'wit battles' with Ben Jonson in the Mermaid Tavern. All of these stories appeared many decades after his death. The only way we will ever really know the author, it seems, is through his works.

RELATED TOPICS
See also
CONTEMPORARY INFLUENCES
page 26

THE AUTHORSHIP QUESTION
page 30

3-SECOND PROMPT
We know both too much and too little about Shakespeare, having dozens of records of his business dealings, but almost nothing personal.

3-MINUTE CALL
Most scholars believe the first allusion to Shakespeare is Robert Greene's 1592 reference to 'the upstart Crow' – an actor who has begun writing blank verse. Greene paraphrases a line from *Henry VI Part Three*, and says the 'Crow' thinks himself 'the only Shake-scene in a country'. But it's possible that 'Shake-scene' simply means 'actor', and Greene's target was actually the famous leading man Edward Alleyn, whose *Tambercam* (an imitation of Marlowe's *Tamburlaine*) was staged that year.

3-SECOND BIOGRAPHIES
ROBERT GREENE
1558–1592
Writer

EDWARD ALLEYN
1566–1626
Actor

BEN JONSON
1572–1637
Writer

30-SECOND TEXT
Ros Barber

In the absence of facts, the Shakespeare legend has grown up around the many myths about the man from Stratford.

RELIGION & POLITICS

the 30-second play

During Shakespeare's lifetime,

religion and politics were closely linked. The 30 years before his birth had seen three changes of official state religion. With the head of state also the head of the church, those not sharing the monarch's religion risked finding themselves declared traitors as well as heretics, and the punishment for treason was death. When Elizabeth ascended the throne in 1558, she promised she would not 'make windows into men's souls'. But after a series of Catholic plots to overthrow her, all nonconformism was considered treasonous. Jesuit priest Edmund Campion was hanged, drawn and quartered for promoting Catholicism. Elizabeth's Catholic cousin, Mary, Queen of Scots, was beheaded. And it was not just Catholics: Puritans Henry Barrow, John Greenwood and John Penry were executed for 'devising and circulating seditious books'. In 1593, religious papers in a room shared by Christopher Marlowe and Thomas Kyd led to both writers being arrested on suspicion of atheism. Kyd was tortured; Marlowe died before he could be prosecuted. 'Shakespeare only became Shakespeare because of the death of Marlowe,' says literary critic Jonathan Bate. 'And he remained peculiarly haunted by that death.' Marlowe directly engaged with the topic of religion in his plays. Perhaps not surprisingly, religious exploration was almost the only aspect of Marlowe's craft that Shakespeare didn't adopt.

RELATED TOPICS
See also
POLITICAL TRANSITION
page 38

BIBLICAL REFERENCES
page 60

3-SECOND PROMPT
In Shakespeare's time, religion was political, and to be outspoken on this issue could be – literally – fatal. Hence perhaps why Shakespeare's plays are resolutely secular.

3-MINUTE CALL
The Church of England was keen to control what Elizabethan audiences watched and read. Theatres were considered immoral places, and churchmen constantly argued for their closure. The Archbishop of Canterbury was chief censor of printed matter. In 1599, he and the Bishop of London ordered that all satires and epigrams, and any histories and dramatic works published without approval, be banned. Of their list of books to be burned, all but one has survived.

3-SECOND BIOGRAPHIES
JOHN WHITGIFT
1530–1604
Archbishop of Canterbury

ST EDMUND CAMPION
1540–1581
Catholic martyr

HENRY BARROW
1550–1593
Puritan separatist

30-SECOND TEXT
Ros Barber

In Elizabeth I's Protestant England, traitors such as Mary, Queen of Scots faced severe punishment.

TEXTUAL SOURCES

the 30-second play

3-SECOND PROMPT
Fact and fiction, past and present writing – Shakespeare read widely and borrowed promiscuously from a wealth of texts to create his plays.

3-MINUTE CALL
Shakespeare's borrowing was never slavish. A character in a source might be a vengeful, murdering bigamist and would-be king, as Amleth was, but Shakespeare's Hamlet is honourable, vulnerable and grief-stricken, a reluctant avenger and an enigma to the last. For *As You Like It* Shakespeare worked differently; he started with Thomas Lodge's *Rosalynde* (1586–1587), discarded all the deaths and most of the physical violence, and added additional family relationships and lovers.

A voracious reader, Shakespeare plundered the books he read for images, names, concepts and plots. More than 270 definite textual sources have been identified, in English, French and Italian, and many others are suspected. His favorite source was probably the Roman poet Ovid, whose *Metamorphoses* was translated into English in 1567. This Shakespeare ransacked for many ideas, including the story of Pyramus and Thisbe for *A Midsummer Night's Dream*. Another ancient text, the Roman Plutarch's *Parallel Lives of the Noble Greeks and Romans* (translated in 1579), lies behind *Antony and Cleopatra* and *Julius Caesar*. But Shakespeare also raided Italian tales, such as Matteo Bandello's *La Prima Parte de la Novelle* (1554) and French stories such as François de Belleforest's *Les Histoires Tragiques* for *Much Ado About Nothing*. Shakespeare borrowed from contemporary fiction too; *The Winter's Tale*'s plot derives mainly from a fellow writer's prose romance, Robert Greene's *Pandosto* (1588), and *Romeo and Juliet* from Arthur Brooke's poem, *The Tragical History of Romeus and Juliet* (1562). But while he was indebted to many texts, Shakespeare's imagination transformed each, creating fresh, original and memorable dramas that both in his time and now capture the minds and emotions of his audiences.

RELATED TOPICS
See also
CLASSICAL INFLUENCES
page 24

LAW
page 66

HISTORY
page 68

3-SECOND BIOGRAPHIES
OVID
43 BCE–17 CE
Latin poet

ARTHUR BROOKE
d.1563
Poet

THOMAS LODGE
1558–1625
Author and physician

30-SECOND TEXT
Margrethe Jolly

Shakespeare found inspiration from a wide range of sources, both ancient and contemporary.

HAMLET

Lear's lack of self-knowledge,

Othello's gullibility, Macbeth's ambition – these personality flaws lead to tragic ends for these great Shakespearean characters. Prince Hamlet is different. He is a student, philosopher and would-be lover with a noble heart, and early in the play he finds himself in an impossible position. A ghost resembling his dead father claims he was murdered by the man now on the throne, his brother Claudius, and wants Hamlet to take revenge. But while the revelation chimes with Hamlet's suspicions of Claudius, to take another's life on the authority of a ghost gives him serious pause for thought. This is a revenge tragedy, once very popular with Elizabethan and Jacobean audiences, and Shakespeare's treatment turns it into a psychological thriller.

The iconic image of a somber Hamlet, often contemplating a skull, conveys instantly the dark, brooding atmosphere of the play. Hamlet is grieving for his father, and repulsed by the rapid remarriage of his mother the Queen to her brother-in-law, a marriage Hamlet sees as incestuous and an implicit betrayal of his father. King Claudius is ruthless and ambitious, and as suspicious of Hamlet as Hamlet is of Claudius. Very soon Hamlet is on guard. Claudius wants to know whether Hamlet's behaviour toward him is prompted by grief for his father, or for other reasons. We watch as the King himself, his counsellor, Ophelia, Hamlet's school-friends Rosencrantz and Guildenstern, and even Hamlet's mother are all engaged to spy on Hamlet and probe his true state of mind.

This constant surveillance has been emphasized in a production at London's National Theatre, giving the play a disconcerting resonance in CCTV Britain. Another production stressed the madness Hamlet seems to adopt to protect himself, though it is Ophelia who finally succumbs to real insanity. However, Claudius will not give up what he has gained by foul means, neither crown nor Queen. His manoeuvres to remove Hamlet become more threatening and confirm his guilt. Hamlet becomes more entrapped, and evasion increasingly difficult. Moments of lightness provide a temporary lifting of the tension; Hamlet's swift wit and equivocation in the Gravedigger scene remind us poignantly of what he is and might have been. But Claudius is too evil and too powerful, Hamlet is mortally wounded, and, at the very end, turns avenger.

Today this revenge tragedy is one of the most frequently performed Shakespearean plays, and Hamlet is a coveted role for major actors.

Margrethe Jolly

CLASSICAL INFLUENCES

the 30-second play

Ben Jonson's *First Folio*

dedication refers to Shakespeare's 'small Latine and lesse Greek', but this is far from truthful. The wide spectrum of classical learning displayed in the canon includes English translations of Ovid's *Metamorphoses*, Homer's *Iliad*, Virgil's *Aeneid*, Plutarch's *Parallel Lives of the Noble Greeks and Romans*, Seneca's *Tenne Tragedies*, Livy's *History of Rome*, Pliny's *Natural History*, Apuleius's *Golden Ass*, the *Aethiopica* of Heliodorus and the comedies of Terence. Scholars have identified numerous classical sources that would have been available only in rare Latin or Greek editions. Plautus's *Menaechmi* and *Amphitryon* influenced *The Comedy of Errors*, and the statue scene of *The Winter's Tale* combines dramaturgy taken from both Ovid's narration of the Pygmalion myth and Euripides's tragicomedy *Alcestis*. Ovid's *Heroides* and *Fasti*, the *Satires* of Juvenal, Latin translations of Plato, Aristotle, Lucian, and the *Greek Anthology* have been identified as sources, leading scholars to assert that Shakespeare read more Latin than classics students do at university today. Some scholars have also argued that his plays reflect intriguing parallels with classical Greek drama, including *The Oresteia* of Aeschylus, Sophocles's *Ajax* and *Oedipus*, Euripides's *Orestes*, *Hecuba*, and *Helen*, and Aristophanes's comedy *Birds*.

RELATED TOPICS
See also
TEXTUAL SOURCES
page 20

GHOSTS
page 122

3-SECOND PROMPT
Shakespeare's classical influences encompass a stunning variety of both Latin and Greek literature, including epic, dramatic, historical, satirical and philosophical texts.

3-MINUTE CALL
Shakespeare seamlessly incorporated a wide spectrum of classical sources in his dramas and poetry in ways that the editors of *Shakespeare and the Uses of Antiquity* (1990) described as 'a miracle we cannot explain'. Despite Ben Jonson's disclaimer and Leonard Digges's *First Folio* poem asserting that Shakespeare did not borrow even 'one phrase' from Greek or Latin, scholars have accumulated evidence that reveals his deep reading of the classics and techniques of imitating classical plots, dramaturgy characterization and philosophy.

3-SECOND BIOGRAPHIES
THOMAS NORTH
1535–1604
Translated Plutarch's *Lives*

ARTHUR GOLDING
1536–1606
Translated Ovid's *Metamorphoses*

THOMAS NEWTON
1542–1607
A translator and poet, edited Seneca's *Tenne Tragedies*

30-SECOND TEXT
Earl Showerman

Numerous references in Shakespeare's work reveal his knowledge of classical writers such as Homer and Euripides.

CONTEMPORARY INFLUENCES

the 30-second play

Dramatic performance was an important part of life in Elizabethan London. Plays were staged in the yards of private inns – notably the Red Bull in Clerkenwell. When James Burbage constructed the first purpose-built theatre (called, aptly, the Theatre) in 1576, others soon followed. The Rose and the Swan were built on the South Bank, where the Globe Theatre was also built (constructed from the timbers of Burbage's original Theatre) in 1599. Plays were performed at Court, at the Inns of Court, and in indoor theatres such as the Blackfriars. The players were well-organized and enjoyed aristocratic or royal patronage. Playwrights fed off each other's work. A popular play would be followed by clear imitations of its style or themes. The trend for revenge drama – epitomized by Thomas Kyd's *The Spanish Tragedy* – inspired *Titus Andronicus* and *Hamlet*. The playwright who most influenced Shakespeare was Christopher Marlowe, whose blank verse line he adopted and adapted, and whose invention of the 'sequel' in *Tamburlaine Part 2* would inspire Shakespeare's multiple Henry plays. Shakespeare's first publication, *Venus and Adonis*, was an epyllion in the style of Marlowe's *Hero and Leander* and his last great creation, Prospero, is the flip-side of Marlowe's Faustus; the name of both magicians means 'fortunate'.

RELATED TOPICS
See also
RELIGION & POLITICS
page 18

TEXTUAL SOURCES
page 20

CLASSICAL INFLUENCES
page 24

3-SECOND BIOGRAPHIES
JAMES BURBAGE
1530/5–1597
Actor and theatre impresario

THOMAS KYD
1558–1594
Dramatist

CHRISTOPHER MARLOWE
1564–1593
Poet and dramatist

30-SECOND TEXT
Ros Barber

Theatre thrived in Elizabethan London with new stages and plays from writers such as Christopher Marlowe.

3-SECOND PROMPT
The variety of playing spaces and audiences in early modern London allowed drama to flourish in a manner that has not been equalled since.

3-MINUTE CALL
Companies from overseas are also recorded in the Elizabethan period. Italian troupes played 'scenario' from the commedia dell'arte for the queen at Windsor. Drousiano, the leader of the most famous troupe called the Gelosi, was even given special dispensation to perform during Lent. Many of Shakespeare's plays, such as *Much Ado About Nothing* and even tragedies such as *Othello*, show the influence of the commedia dell'arte in setting, plot and character.

THE SONNETS

the 30-second play

3-SECOND PROMPT
The sonnet existed in both Italian and English long before Shakespeare wrote one, yet he made the form entirely his own. The sonnets are among his most popular work.

3-MINUTE CALL
Who is the mysterious 'Mr W.H.' to whom the sonnets are addressed, described as their 'onlie begetter'? Suggestions include William Herbert, a dedicatee of the *First Folio*, and a (reversed) Henry Wriothesley, to whom *Venus and Adonis* is addressed, but neither earl would have been addressed as 'Mr'. A typo for the author, 'W. SH'? Or could it stand for 'Mr Who He'? This mystery is the subject of Oscar Wilde's short story *The Portrait of Mr. W. H.*

'Shall I compare thee to a summer's day?' begins the eighteenth of Shakespeare's sonnets, first published in 1609. Nobody knows the addressee of this or any of the other 154 sonnets; they include a 'dark lady', a 'fair youth', and quite possibly others, none of whom we can identify with any certainty. The apparent impossibility of linking the sonnets to anything (or anyone) in Shakespeare's known life has led some scholars to conclude that they are not autobiographical. And yet, full of heartfelt emotion, they don't feel like a writing exercise. Shakespeare describes a triangular relationship with an unknown beloved and a 'rival poet', bemoans some 'shame' or 'disgrace' that has befallen him, and in Sonnet 66, even appears to be suicidal: 'Tired of all this, for restful death I cry.' Against the conventions of his time, he is wickedly rude toward the 'dark lady'; and some scholars read from the sonnets hints of bisexuality and treatment for venereal disease. Whether the characters are real or fictional, the sonnets represent a powerful poetic achievement, allowing him full rein in both playfulness (including puns) and in imagery. He set new standards for the form – particularly in the love sonnets – as well as a new standard rhyme scheme: the Shakespearean sonnet, abab/cdcd/efef/gg.

RELATED TOPICS
See also
THE AUTHORSHIP QUESTION
page 30

RHYME
page 80

3-SECOND BIOGRAPHIES
HENRY WRIOTHESLEY
1573–1624
3rd Earl of Southampton

WILLIAM HERBERT
1580–1630
3rd Earl of Pembroke

OSCAR WILDE
1854–1900
Writer

30-SECOND TEXT
Ros Barber

Some of the sonnets are addressed to a mysterious 'fair youth' and a 'dark lady'.

THE AUTHORSHIP QUESTION

the 30-second play

RELATED TOPICS
See also
THE LIFE & LEGEND
page 16

THE SONNETS
page 28

3-SECOND BIOGRAPHIES
DELIA BACON
1811–1859
Author of *The Philosophy of the Plays of Shakespeare Unfolded*

FRIEDRICH NIETZSCHE
1844–1900
German philosopher and poet

SIGMUND FREUD
1856–1939
Founder of psychoanalysis

30-SECOND TEXT
Ros Barber

3-SECOND PROMPT
Does it matter who wrote the plays and poems we know as Shakespeare's? With insufficient evidence on either side, the question may never be resolved.

3-MINUTE CALL
A fine example of the frustrating absence of evidence around William Shakespeare is his lodger, Thomas Greene. Greene and his wife lived in the Shakespeare family home in Stratford from 1603 to 1611. Greene (a lawyer) was a published poet and diarist – yet even though he was living in Shakespeare's home in 1609, the year *Shakespeares Sonnets* were published, the scraps of his diary that survive only mention 'cousin Shakespeare' in relation to land deals.

By the 1850s, all major documents relating to William Shakespeare of Stratford-upon-Avon had been discovered, and the historical record proved disturbingly prosaic. Some people found the documentary evidence of his life entirely at odds with their sense of the author of the plays and poems. Delia Bacon was the first to raise the question openly: was William Shakespeare of Stratford really the author of the works attributed to him? Would the author of so many strong, educated female characters really leave both his daughters functionally illiterate? Why have no letters, books or manuscripts survived from William Shakespeare, when all other major writers of the period have left some trace? Why does his will mention nothing related to a literary life, not so much as a bookcase or a desk? Was the man we think of as the greatest English author actually a play-broker, or a 'front' for some other author or group of authors? Most scholars take a dim view of 'anti-Stratfordians' but doubters of Shakespeare's authorship include the father of psychoanalysis, Sigmund Freud, and the philosopher Friedrich Nietzsche. As a conflict of beliefs, the debate can take on a religious flavour: Shakespeare doubt is referred to as heresy. To many, to question Shakespeare's authorship is like questioning the existence of God.

Francis Bacon, William Stanley, Christopher Marlowe, Edward de Vere and Mary Sidney have all been proposed as alternative authors of Shakespeare's works.

CO-AUTHORSHIP

the 30-second play

As early as 1687 critics began blaming other authors for lines or entire works that they perceived as unworthy of Shakespeare's genius and his assumed kind and gentle nature. There are various indications in a number of Shakespeare's plays that someone else acted as co-author or reviser, or provided additional matter, sometimes as individual lines or even as entire interpolated scenes, mainly in the very early and late plays. Thomas Middleton is thought to have meddled with *Macbeth*, *Measure for Measure* and *Timon of Athens*; John Fletcher may have had a hand in *Henry VIII*; George Peele may have contributed to *Titus Andronicus*; there are perhaps signs that Thomas Nashe involved himself in *Henry VI Part One*. Scholars have used a wide range of technical tests including rare word use, contractions, word length, syllables per word, distribution of parts of speech, first words, use of rhyme, proportion of blank verse to prose, lines with an eleventh syllable, Latinate vocabulary and many other complex techniques in the quest to determine exactly what Shakespeare himself wrote. No authorship test, however, can prove whether or not Shakespeare sat down as a willing co-author on any play, only that others may have involved themselves with the text.

RELATED TOPICS
See also
CONTEMPORARY INFLUENCES
page 26

THE AUTHORSHIP QUESTION
page 30

APOCRYPHA
page 148

3-SECOND BIOGRAPHIES
GEORGE PEELE
1556–1596
Elizabethan dramatist

THOMAS NASHE
1567–c.1601
Elizabethan satirist

THOMAS MIDDLETON
1580–1627
Jacobean poet and playwright

30-SECOND TEXT
Robin Williams

3-SECOND PROMPT
Because Shakespeare's works have been edited, rewritten, cut and modernized, thousands of editors, actors and directors can be considered Shakespeare's 'coauthors'.

3-MINUTE CALL
Co-authorship studies have 'proven' that the anonymous play *Edward III* was written by George Peele alone; by Christopher Marlowe with George Peele, Robert Greene and Thomas Kyd; by Thomas Kyd alone; by Michael Drayton; by Robert Wilson; by William Shakespeare alone; by Shakespeare and one unknown other; by Shakespeare and Marlowe; by Shakespeare and several others, excluding Marlowe; and that Shakespeare wrote 60 percent and Kyd 40 percent.

Thomas Middleton and John Fletcher are thought to be two of Shakespeare's 'co-authors'.

THEMES

THEMES
GLOSSARY

Arden The name of the forest to which Duke Senior and his followers are exiled in *As You Like It*. There was a Forest of Arden in Shakespeare's home county Warwickshire, but the play's setting comes from the source story, which was set in Ardennes, France.

Bohemia A historical country of central Europe, located in what is now the Czech Republic. Its capital was Prague.

bed-trick A deception whereby two women trade places in order to trick a man into sleeping with one of them, while believing he is sleeping with the other (usually requiring total darkness).

Desdemona The tragic heroine of Shakespeare's *Othello*; Othello's wife.

dramatic irony A literary technique originating in Greek drama, whereby the full significance of a character's words and actions are unknown to them, but clear to the audience.

Essex Rebellion The name given to the attempt of the 2nd Earl of Essex, Robert Devereux, to speak to Queen Elizabeth I (to protest at her treatment of him, which included house arrest) by descending upon her court with 200 followers, many of them armed. He was subsequently executed.

Falstaff A major comic character in *Henry IV Part One*; a cowardly carousing knight who leads Prince Hal astray. He has a small part in *Henry IV Part Two* (where Hal rejects him) and features again in the comedy *The Merry Wives of Windsor*.

history play A play that is based on real historical events.

Iago A character in Shakespeare's *Othello*; Othello's standard-bearer, who persuades him that his wife, Desdemona, is unfaithful.

metaphor A figure of speech in which one thing is compared directly to another by saying it is that thing e.g., 'life is but a walking shadow'.

Moor In Shakespeare's era 'Moor' was a term usually used to describe North African Muslims.

Othello One of Shakespeare's most famous tragedies, and the name of its main character.

Plantagenet The Plantagenet family (who were French in origin) ruled England from the accession of Henry II in 1154 to the death of Richard III in 1485, when they were replaced by the Tudors.

problem play Shakespeare's 'problem plays' are those in which there are violent shifts between dark, psychological drama and light comedy. Originally applied to *All's Well That Ends Well*, *Measure for Measure* and *Troilus and Cressida*, it has since been extended to others including *The Winter's Tale* and *Timon of Athens*.

slander A false spoken statement damaging to a person's reputation.

Star Chamber An English court of law made up of Privy Councillors (the queen's advisors) as well as judges, which sat at the Palace of Westminster. It held hearings in secret, with no witnesses.

succession The royal succession: the act of one monarch following another.

tetralogy A work of four parts (whereas a trilogy is a work of three parts).

usurp To take the place of someone in a position of power illegally or by force.

POLITICAL TRANSITION

the 30-second play

3-SECOND PROMPT
Shakespeare's history plays provided him with a safe vehicle to explore the dangerous subject of succession, and the relationship between ruler and ruled.

3-MINUTE CALL
On the eve of the 1601 Essex Rebellion, followers of the Earl of Essex paid Shakespeare's company 40 shillings to stage *Richard II*, which contains a scene where the monarch is deposed by one of his Earls. Elizabeth I declared to her archivist 'I am Richard II, know you not that?' Essex and many of his followers were executed. Shakespeare's company were called to explain themselves, but Shakespeare didn't appear, and, unlike John Hayward, was never punished.

Political transition was a sensitive subject in the late 16th century. When it became clear that Queen Elizabeth I was not going to produce an heir, succession became a hot topic – and a banned one. The fate of John Stubbs, whose right hand was chopped off when he wrote a pamphlet against the queen's marriage (saying that, aged 46, she was too old to have children) was a clear warning not to write directly about the succession. But historical drama proved a safer channel, and Shakespeare addressed the topical issue of political transition time and again through his history plays. Dramatizing history was far safer than documenting it: John Hayward, the author of a historical treatise that covered the same ground as Shakespeare's *Richard II*, was prosecuted in the Star Chamber, and imprisoned. By contrast, Shakespeare freely explored the rights, powers and duties of monarchy, and repeatedly focused on the transfer of power. In the *Henry VI* plays, Shakespeare effectively warned against the distressing results of the civil war that can result from a tumultuous transition, including a son accidentally killing his father, and vice versa. Half a century later, the arrogance of King Charles I, son of the king who adopted Shakespeare's company, caused England to descend again into civil war, closing the theatres for nearly two decades.

RELATED TOPICS
See also
RELIGION & POLITICS
Page 18

USURPATION
page 40

3-SECOND BIOGRAPHIES
JOHN STUBBS
1543–1591
Pamphleteer

JOHN HAYWARD
1564–1627
Author of *The Life and Reign of King Henry IV*

ROBERT DEVEREUX
1565–1601
2nd Earl of Essex

30-SECOND TEXT
Ros Barber

Writing about contemporary politics was too risky, so Shakespeare turned to history to explore the theme of transition.

USURPATION

the 30-second play

Shakespeare's interest in

usurpers begins with British history: in his early tetralogy, Henry VI is accused of being a usurper by the Duke of York and the rebel Jack Cade because his grandfather, Henry IV (featured in Shakespeare's later tetralogy) stole the crown from Richard II. Henry VI is then usurped by Edward, Duke of York whose son is, in turn, usurped by Richard III. *Macbeth* hinges on the usurpation of King Duncan. *King John* is another usurper. Not only nobles are usurped in these plays: a petitioner protests that one John Goodman has kept 'my house, my lands, and wife and all, from me'. But Shakespeare continues the theme beyond the plots of British history. In *As You Like It*, Duke Senior lives in the forest after being usurped by his brother Frederick. In *The Tempest*, the arch-usurper Antonio has not only illegally supplanted Prospero as Duke of Milan, but also persuades Sebastian to murder and usurp his brother King Alonso. The trigger event of *Hamlet* is Claudius usurping his brother's throne and wife. The author plays with the word even as Horatio challenges the dead king's ghost: 'What art thou that usurp'st this time of night?' And Lucianus, playing Gonzago's murderer in the play intended to 'catch the King' instructs the poison 'On wholesome life usurp immediately'.

RELATED TOPICS
See also
HAMLET
page 22

POLITICAL TRANSITION
page 38

FALSE ACCUSATION
page 42

MACBETH
page 104

3-SECOND PROMPT
Many of Shakespeare's histories and tragedies – and even some comedies – hinge upon someone taking a position of power illegally or by force.

3-MINUTE CALL
Shakespeare often used the word 'usurp' as a metaphor. In *Henry VI Part One*, Lord Talbot says he who is not fearless 'Doth but usurp the sacred name of knight.' In *All's Well That Ends Well*, Bertram says of cowardly soldier Parolles, 'resting' in the stocks: 'his heels have deserved it, in usurping his spurs so long.' When King Lear dies, Kent says 'The wonder is, he hath endur'd so long. He but usurp'd his life.'

3-SECOND BIOGRAPHIES
MAC BETHAD MAC FINDLAÍCH, OR MACBETH
c.1005–1057
King of Scotland

KING HENRY IV
1367–1413
King of England

RICHARD III
1452–1485
Last Plantagenet king of England

30-SECOND TEXT
Ros Barber

The death of Richard II is one of the many bloody usurpations represented in Shakespeare's plays.

FALSE ACCUSATION

the 30-second play

The motif of an honourable

person slandered or falsely accused recurs throughout Shakespeare's plays. With women, the false slur is always against their chastity or fidelity. In *Much Ado About Nothing*, Don John persuades Claudio that his fiancée Hero is unfaithful. Denounced in public on her wedding day, she faints so profoundly that she is believed to be 'slandered to death'. In *The Winter's Tale*, Leontes publicly accuses his wife Hermione of infidelity. Their son Mamillius dies of a wasting illness brought on by these accusations, their baby daughter grows up in exile and the wronged wife pretends to be dead for 16 years. In *Cymbeline*, Iachimo convinces Posthumus he has seduced Imogen, and Posthumus sends a servant to murder her. All these women are lucky enough to survive their slander; *Othello*'s Desdemona is less fortunate. When men suffer false accusation it is related to honour and power. In *King Lear*, Gloucester's illegitimate son Edmund fools his father into thinking his legitimate son, Edgar, is planning to kill him. Edgar loses everything – including his name – but guides his blinded father and prevents his suicide. *Richard II* opens with Mowbray and Bolingbroke swapping accusations they each claim are false. Bolingbroke's recovery of his honour includes deposing his king.

RELATED TOPICS
See also
USURPATION
page 40

OTHELLO
page 44

REPUTATION
page 50

3-SECOND PROMPT
Slander is a great plot-driver for Shakespeare. In the comedies, truth and honour usually triumph, but false accusation also leads to tragedy and death.

3-MINUTE CALL
Shakespeare's works feature the word 'slander' nearly 100 times, and not only in the plays. In the Sonnets, one speaks of 'maiden virtue rudely strumpeted, / And right perfection wrongfully disgraced' (66), and another on the subject of 'slander's mark' states 'That thou art blamed shall not be thy defect' (70). The poet speaks of 'those blots that do with me remain' (36) and of being 'in disgrace' (29), concluding 'Tis better to be vile than vile esteemed' (121).

30-SECOND TEXT
Ros Barber

Iago's false accusations against Desdemona's virtue leads to her tragic murder by Othello.

OTHELLO

You are a well-respected, if a little rough around the edges, army general. You have married Desdemona, a beautiful girl who is much younger than you, without her father's knowledge or permission. He disapproves of you because you are a Moor, black, an outsider in culture and class. Your wife speaks up for you, publicly, when her father accuses you of enchanting her into marriage. She is a young woman who knows her own mind and acts upon it. Then Iago, your trusted ensign, tells you that Desdemona is having an affair with your young, courtly lieutenant, Cassio. Do you believe him? How much proof would you need?

In *Othello*, Shakespeare explores the workings of jealousy and revenge. Iago initiates his plot to discredit Desdemona to take his revenge on Othello for promoting Cassio before him and, he later adds, because he believes Othello has slept with his wife, Emilia. The speed at which Iago is able to work Othello from utmost trust in his wife to maddening jealousy and her murder is perplexing for many. He plays heavily on Othello's own insecurities in age and difference, but this is not, perhaps, enough. As Othello points out, his wife 'had eyes' when she chose him. Some see Iago as a kind of devil, revelling in the pain and mischief he causes, leading Othello from heaven (in love) to hell (in murder-suicide). For others, Iago's insinuations and careful manipulation of characters and evidence are supported by Desdemona's flirtatiousness, strong-mindedness, and outspokenness in a society that equates female silence with female chastity. Driven to the point of madness in his jealousy, Othello suffocates his wife. She revives just long enough to blame herself for her death, and then dies. A last, dutiful act of loyalty to Othello, or a dramatic warning to outspoken, independent young women in a society that expects obedience to fathers and silence in public? The death of Emilia for speaking out against her husband's villainy does little to resolve the questions raised by Desdemona's self-blame.

Learning of Iago's trickery, Othello draws parallels between himself and the Turkish enemy he had travelled to Cyprus (the setting of most of the action) to fight. He then commits suicide. While the play invites us to consider issues of race, gender, class and love, Othello's final speech and action raise questions about how well we know each other and ourselves.

Jessica Dyson

RESURRECTION

the 30-second play

Whether Shakespeare's love of
resurrection was inspired by the central tenet
of Christianity, or simply due to its being a
powerful dramatic device that can fire the
engine of both comedy and tragedy, the
playwright loved to bring people back from the
dead. Thirty-three characters in 18 of his plays
are wrongly thought to be dead for anything
from a few seconds to almost all of the action.
With Henry IV, Cleopatra, and Desdemona,
it's just a case of prematurity. But the key
characters of *The Tempest* – including Prospero,
Miranda, Ferdinand and Alonso – are all
presumed to be dead (by others in the play)
until the very end. Presumed death at sea is the
most frequent cause of happy resurrections:
in addition to *The Tempest*, *Twelfth Night*,
A Comedy of Errors and *Pericles* all feature
non-drownings in their plots. Several characters
actually fake their death, usually to get out of
trouble: *Much Ado*'s Hero, *All's Well*'s Helena,
Cymbeline's Imogen, *Measure for Measure*'s
Claudio and *Henry IV*'s Falstaff. Juliet fakes her
death to get out of marrying Paris, and tragically
loses Romeo to suicide as a consequence. But
more often resurrection scenes mark the happy
endings of comedies, where twins and family
members are reunited.

3-SECOND PROMPT
Shakespeare popularized
tales of the living dead long
before the current vogue
for zombies and vampires.

3-MINUTE CALL
Hermione's resurrection
from a lifelike statue at
the end of *The Winter's
Tale* is considered one
of Shakespeare's most
astonishing scenes. Having
supposedly died of a
broken heart while on trial
for adultery and treason
16 years earlier, her return
to life can be read either as
a miracle or as a trick. The
resurrection was not in
Shakespeare's source,
Robert Greene's *Pandosto*;
his splicing a happy ending
onto this tragedy makes it
a 'problem play'.

RELATED TOPICS
See also
MISTAKEN IDENTITY
page 48

ELIZABETHAN MAGIC
page 118

CHARMS & POTIONS
page 130

3-SECOND BIOGRAPHIES
SIR JOHN OLDCASTLE
d.1417
The original name of Falstaff

ROBERT GREENE
1558–1592
Dramatist and early novelist

30-SECOND TEXT
Ros Barber

*Hermione is resurrected
from a statue; other
characters are believed
to be lost at sea or use
poison to fake death.*

MISTAKEN IDENTITY
the 30-second play

RELATED TOPICS
See also
USURPATION
page 40

STRONG WOMEN
page 108

30-SECOND TEXT
Ros Barber

3-SECOND PROMPT
The comedy and drama that arise from mistaken identity force us to confront what is real, and what imagined, about the roles we routinely inhabit.

3-MINUTE CALL
Shakespeare twice uses the 'bed-trick', a mistaken-identity-driven plot device that goes back to the Old Testament. *Measure for Measure*'s Angelo, refusing to honour his betrothal to Mariana because her dowry was lost at sea, pursues Isabella; Isabella agrees to submit to him in darkness, but lets Mariana take her place. In *All's Well That Ends Well*, Bertram unknowingly consummates his forced marriage with Helena, thinking he is sleeping with someone else.

Shakespeare's plays are full of one person being taken for another. Sometimes this is accidental: *The Comedy of Errors* features, implausibly, two pairs of identically named twins. More often, this is due to deliberate disguise. Cross-dressing allows *Twelfth Night*'s Viola, disguised as Cesario, to be mistaken for her twin brother Sebastian. *As You Like It*'s Rosalind, disguised as a man, is unrecognized by Orlando, who purports to love her. Portia (*The Merchant of Venice*) disguises herself as a 'doctor of law' in order to save her husband's friend. In a double-layered case of mistaken identity *Cymbeline*'s Imogen (disguised as a boy) thinks the headless body of her would-be rapist is that of her husband. In *The Merry Wives of Windsor*, Falstaff dresses as a woman to escape a jealous husband, and both Justice Slender and Doctor Caius elope mistakenly with young boys instead of the female object of their desire. Mistaken identity often drives comedy, but it creates poignancy in the tragedies. Edgar, disguised as Tom O'Bedlam in *King Lear*, goes unrecognized by Lear, Lear's fool, and his blinded father Gloucester. In *Julius Caesar*, the mob murder Cinna the poet, mistaking him for Cinna the conspirator. And when Hamlet stabs Ophelia's father Polonius, thinking he is killing Claudius, he sows the seed of his own death.

Cross-dressing and identical twins are common plot devices in Shakespeare's comedies.

REPUTATION

the 30-second play

3-SECOND PROMPT
Playing on concepts of reputation allows Shakespeare to explore relationships of trust and ideas of intrinsic and constructed identity.

3-MINUTE CALL
While characters often become first known to audiences by reputation, Shakespeare's exploration of character and identity through reputation goes beyond an easy matching of the two: Prince Hal actively cultivates a bad reputation so that, when he becomes king, his true self will seem so much better, and it is deceitful Iago's reputation as 'honest' that allows him to drive Othello mad with jealousy.

Shakespeare is interested in the power of reputation: how it makes people respond to others; how important it may be to posterity. In his plays, 'the bubble reputation' is hard won and easily lost. Caught, just once, drunk and fighting, Othello's lieutenant Cassio laments bitterly the loss of his good reputation, seeing it as the 'immortal part' of himself, an identity living outside and beyond his mortal body. For others, reputation is a more immediate marker of identity. In *Antony and Cleopatra*, Antony wrestles with his identity in his love for Cleopatra, attempting to revive his dwindling authority through reputation, claiming 'I am Antony yet!' *Henry VI*'s Talbot has such a fearsome reputation that crying his name alone is an effective weapon, and in *Henry IV*, Hotspur's valiant military reputation leads the king to wish his son had been swapped at birth, since Prince Hal has a reputation only for debauchery. The undeserved loss of a chaste reputation causes serious difficulties for female characters who, like Imogen (*Cymbeline*) and Hero (*Much Ado About Nothing*) are threatened with the loss of a spouse and undergo an ordeal until the slander is proven unfounded. Audiences are often in a privileged position, hearing of the reputation and seeing the truth, enabling Shakespeare to build tension through dramatic irony.

RELATED TOPICS
See also
FALSE ACCUSATION
page 42

OTHELLO
page 44

FIGHTERS
page 102

3-SECOND BIOGRAPHIES
SIR HENRY 'HOTSPUR' PERCY
1364–1403
English nobleman who led an uprising against King Henry IV

JOHN TALBOT
1387–1453
1st Earl of Shrewsbury

30-SECOND TEXT
Jessica Dyson

Shakespeare explores the importance of reputation – and the loss of it – to his characters' identities.

EXILE

the 30-second play

More than 20 characters in

Shakespeare's works are exiled; some, such as Prospero and Miranda (The Tempest) from the outset and others, such as Valentine (*Two Gentlemen of Verona*) during the action. Shakespeare explores the agonies of exile in detail in *Richard II* and *Romeo and Juliet*: Thomas Mowbray is horrified to lose his use of native English, saying 'now my tongue's use is to me no more / Than an unstringed viol or a harp', and when Romeo is told he is banished from Verona, he tells Friar Laurence 'Be merciful, say "death".' Banishment is seen as a harsh punishment, often inflicted on Shakespeare's heroes and heroines unjustly. Kent (*King Lear*) is banished for being the only one of Lear's advisers prepared to tell him the truth; Posthumus (*Cymbeline*) is banished for loving Imogen; Perdita (*The Winter's Tale*), while only a baby, is sent to the seacoast of Bohemia, and grows up in exile because her mother was wrongly accused of adultery. But some exiles emerge triumphant. Perdita falls in love in Bohemia. And exile to the forest of Arden, according to Duke Senior (*As You Like It*) is 'more free from peril than the envious court'. He declares he finds 'sermons in stones, and good in everything. I would not change it.'

3-SECOND PROMPT

Shakespeare was fascinated by the drama of exile, which leads either to revenge and tragedy, or to pastoral frolicking from which the exiles emerge triumphant.

3-MINUTE CALL

In *Henry IV Part One*, in a piece of play-acting, Falstaff begs Prince Hal (who is playing his father) not to banish him: 'Banish plump Jack, and banish all the world.' But in the final scene of *Henry IV Part Two*, Hal – now king – banishes Falstaff to stay ten miles from him, saying 'I have turned away my former self.' Hal's movement into and out of the Eastcheap underworld functions like the pastoral exiles of other plays.

RELATED TOPICS

See also
TEXTUAL SOURCES
page 20

FALSE ACCUSATION
page 42

REPUTATION
page 50

30-SECOND TEXT
Ros Barber

Banishment and exile were a common theme in Shakespeare's dramas. Prospero and Miranda are forced to live in exile in The Tempest.

KNOWLEDGE

alchemy An early chemistry concerned with trying to convert substances into one another, with a particular focus on turning base metals into gold or a life-giving elixir.

allegory A story or poem with a meaning that can be applied more generally to reveal truths about human existence or which tells another story in a veiled form.

allusion An indirect reference intended to bring something to mind without mentioning it explicitly.

apocryphal Of doubtful authenticity, though circulated as being true.

Barbary A region on the Mediterranean coast of northern Africa.

Bohemia A historical country of central Europe, located in what is now the Czech Republic. Its capital was Prague.

Cordelia King Lear's youngest daughter.

Corinth An ancient city-state on the isthmus of Corinth, which joined the Peloponnesus to the mainland of Greece.

Exodus The second book of the Old Testament, in which Moses leads the Jews out of Egypt in search of the Promised Land, parting the Red Sea and receiving the Ten Commandments.

four humours The four fluids of the body which, it was believed, needed to be balanced for a person to be healthy, according to the system of Ancient Greek medicine still popular in Elizabethan England. The four humours (and temperaments) were blood (sanguine), yellow bile (choleric), black bile (melancholic), and phlegm (phlegmatic).

Genesis The first book of the Old Testament, in which God creates the earth in six days (including Adam and Eve).

Goneril King Lear's eldest (and villainous) daughter.

history play A play that is based on real historical events.

King Lear One of Shakespeare's most successful tragedies, and the name of its main character.

Levant The Eastern Mediterranean, nowadays comprising Cyprus, Israel, Jordan, Lebanon, Palestine, Syria and part of southern Turkey.

Macedonia An ancient Balkan country established as a province by the Romans and situated between the countries of Albania, Bulgaria and Greece.

physiology The scientific study of function in living systems.

Regan King Lear's second eldest (and villainous) daughter.

Renaissance From the word for 'rebirth', a cultural movement spanning the 14th to 17th centuries that encompassed a flowering of knowledge as well as literature and art based on classical (i.e. Ancient Roman and Greek) models. Beginning in Italy, it was partially assisted by the increased availability of paper and the invention of movable type.

Shakespeare canon The whole body of literary and dramatic works (poems and plays) written by Shakespeare.

Tudor The Tudor family ruled England from the accession of Henry VII in 1485 to the death of Elizabeth I in 1603, when they were replaced by the Stuarts.

LANGUAGE & VOCABULARY

the 30-second play

Elizabethan London was a cosmopolitan city, abuzz with foreign traders and ambassadors. Shakespeare's plays reflect his excitement in encountering and borrowing from other cultures and languages. Exactly how proficient he was in Latin, Italian and French, and perhaps Greek and Spanish, is undecided, but these languages are vital sources for the plays' settings, characters' names, and vocabulary. Shakespeare offers us, for instance, culture-specific terms such as 'chopines' in *Hamlet* (Italian shoes that raised the wearer up to one-and-a-half feet – about 50cm – above the debris littering the streets), audaciously long words such as 'honorificabilitudinitatibus', and a mock Latin lesson in *Love's Labours Lost*. He might even be the first user of 'franglais' in his blend of French and English in *Henry V*, where the French princess is learning English: 'le col, de nick' (the neck), 'le menton, de sin' (the chin). Was Shakespeare's vocabulary exceptional, as some have claimed? Recent investigations by Ward E. Y. Elliott and Robert J. Valenza show he *used* some 30,000 different words in his plays and poems, and probably *knew* at least as many more; his total vocabulary approximates to that of a modern educated person. But Shakespeare's language still impresses us, because of his range of topics, his accessibility and his freshness of expression.

RELATED TOPICS
See also
TEXTUAL SOURCES
page 20

GEOGRAPHY
page 70

TURNS OF PHRASE
page 84

30-SECOND TEXT
Margrethe Jolly

3-SECOND PROMPT
Shakespeare revelled in the Renaissance's linguistic riches but valued native English too, as in Falstaff's insults, describing Prince Hal as a 'stock-fish' and 'bull-pizzle.'

3-MINUTE CALL
Shakespeare is constantly alert to the ambiguities and potential in vocabulary. He can use formal, Latinate words like 'honourable' and 'ambitious' ironically in Mark Antony's famous speech, but he also plays with sexual innuendo, with English names such as Mistress Overdone (a 'Bawd') in *Measure for Measure*, and Doll Tearsheet in *Henry IV Part Two*. And when Romeo hears the fatally wounded Mercutio say that tomorrow he will be 'a grave man', Shakespeare's punned again.

The language in the plays reflects the cosmopolitan makeup of Elizabethan London.

opir

le col, de ni

le menton, de sin

onourable

stock-fish

orificabilitudinitatibus

BIBLICAL REFERENCES

the 30-second play

RELATED TOPICS
See also
RELIGION & POLITICS
page 18

RESURRECTION
page 46

GHOSTS
page 122

3-SECOND PROMPT
Among the Biblical allusions, Shakespeare effortlessly weaves in the gods of ancient Greek, Roman and Celtic mythology.

3-MINUTE CALL
It has been claimed that Shakespeare's works indicate variously that he was a secret Catholic, disliked Catholics, was Jewish, had Jesuit leanings, was a conforming Anglican Christian or New Age humanist, was interested in Buddhism, or that he had no religion whatsoever. His allusions provide verbal echoes of both Protestant and Catholic versions of the Bible and also include philosophical ideas that conflict with both theologies, making it difficult to assume anything about his personal beliefs.

The Bible was a powerful cultural influence in Shakespeare's time. Scholars have found more than 2,000 Biblical echoes of varying degrees in his plays. The more obvious references are frequently ambiguous and often provocative. What are we to make of Bolingbroke comparing himself to God in *Richard II* when he claims that the blood of a murdered man calls to him from the ground, as Abel's blood calls to God in Genesis? When the villain Iago declares, 'I am not what I am', is there significance in the reversal of God's message to Moses, 'I am that I am' in Exodus? Richard III boasts that he 'clothes his naked villainy / With odd old ends, stolen forth of Holy Writ' – does this imply a connection between religion and corruption of power? Shakespeare expects his audience to be familiar with the Bible, as in the references to the two Daniels in *The Merchant of Venice* that depend on a knowledge of the 'second Daniel' in the apocryphal book, Susanna. Some claim *The Tempest* is an allegory of Genesis, others that it is an allegory of the Apocalypse. The multiple interpretations possible in the Biblical allusions provide extraordinary elements for discussion.

3-SECOND BIOGRAPHY
WILLIAM TYNDALE
c.1494–1536
Printed the first New Testament in English in 1526 and was burned at the stake for it in Antwerp

30-SECOND TEXT
Robin Williams

References to the Bible occur throughout Shakespeare's work.

MEDICINE

the 30-second play

3-SECOND PROMPT
The depth of medical knowledge and favourable representation of physicians displayed in Shakespeare's plays is unique and has intrigued physicians and scholars for more than a century.

3-MINUTE CALL
Shakespeare used medical imagery far more often than his contemporaries and had a keen sense of the correct use of medical terminology, providing clinical descriptions unsurpassed in their erudition. In *Mad Folk in Shakespeare* (1867), psychiatrist John Charles Bucknill commented, 'That abnormal states of mind were a favourite study of Shakespeare would be evident from the mere number of characters to which he has attributed them, and to the extent alone to which he has written on the subject.'

Physicians and literary scholars have long recognized the medical knowledge reflected in the Shakespeare canon to be extraordinary. Studies have confirmed Shakespeare was familiar with contemporary medical practices and literature, including books on anatomy, physiology, surgery, alchemy, infectious disease, psychology and Hippocratic methods. While Shakespeare's medical acumen is noteworthy, what sets him apart from other playwrights is his admiring, sympathetic representation of physicians and empiric healers as dramatic characters. According to the *British Medical Journal*, 'he loved them, his large mind saw the nobility of medicine's aim.' Lord Cerimon (*Pericles*) and Helena (*All's Well That Ends Well*) possess near-magical healing powers, while Friar Laurence (*Romeo and Juliet*) and Cornelius (*Cymbeline*) are able to concoct potions that virtually suspend life. Only Doctor Pinch (*Comedy of Errors*) and Doctor Caius (*The Merry Wives of Windsor*) are satirized in the manner commonly practised by other Elizabethan playwrights. More than 700 medical allusions have been identified in the plays, with many references to Galen's doctrine of the four humours, and a wide array of clinical topics, including neurology, psychiatry, toxicology, Paracelsian homeopathy and forensics.

RELATED TOPICS
See also
TEXTUAL SOURCES
page 20

RESURRECTION
page 46

CHARMS & POTIONS
page 130

3-SECOND BIOGRAPHIES
THOMAS ELYOT
1490–1546
Physician and author of
The Castle of Health

THOMAS VICARY
1490–1561
Physician and author of
Anatomy of the Body of Man

GEORGE BAKER
1540–1600
Surgeon and author of
New Jewel of Health

30-SECOND TEXT
Earl Showerman

His plays display a keen understanding of medicine, although how Shakespeare gained this knowledge is a mystery.

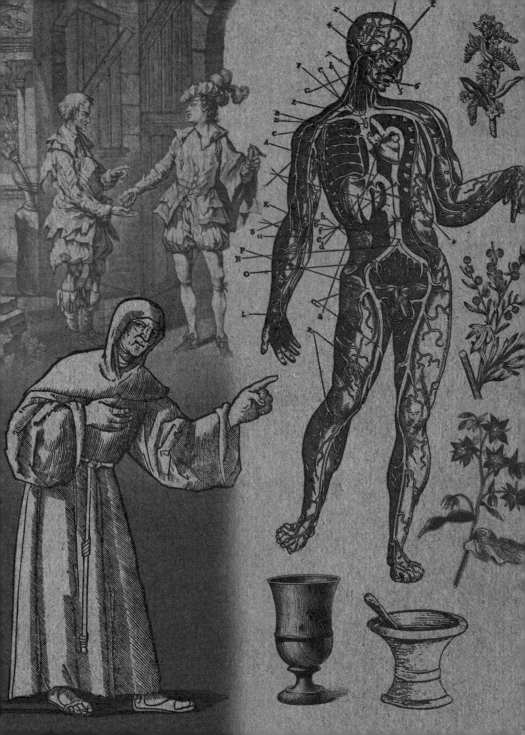

KING LEAR

King Lear begins as an uneasy amalgamation between a history play and a folktale but ends as Shakespeare's bleakest tragedy. It seems at first that the enmity between the king's sons-in-law, the Dukes of Albany and Cornwall, will dominate the action as old King Lear decides to abdicate and divide the kingdom between his children. Lear then initiates a love test for his three daughters, Goneril, Regan and Cordelia. He banishes Cordelia, the youngest, most beloved and most truthful, because she will not flatter her father with insincerity. As in all good stories, Lear's vanity and folly must be punished before a loving reunion can be achieved but the forces unleashed by Lear's question – 'which of you … doth love us most?' – are so unstoppable that the kingdom is destroyed: madness, barbarity, civil war and invasion ensue; and the good, as well as the evil and the foolish, suffer and die.

Need, necessity and excess dominate the play. Lear needs to know that he's loved but vainly thinks that love can be measured. He foolishly equates excessive words and true emotion, failing to realize that *saying* nothing doesn't mean *feeling* nothing. The gorgeous robes of majesty and the formal ceremonial of court – the excesses of Lear's kingliness – are stripped away to expose bare humanity. Lear goes mad and, shut out from all he knows and loves, he rages at the violent storm that expresses his confusion and makes him understand his own human needs. Fellow-feelings of estrangement, isolation, suffering and exclusion are experienced in the company of his Fool, a servant, a beggar and a blind man. In Lear's daughters, Goneril and Regan, the humanity that's revealed is grasping, cruel and vengeful. They turn on their father and each other, completing the destructive work begun by Lear. Excessively, Shakespeare provides a double-plot involving another father – Gloucester – and his two sons, Edmund and Edgar. As 'bastard' Edmund plots against 'legitimate' Edgar, another family is destroyed and Gloucester is blinded in one of Shakespeare's most horrifying scenes.

The longed-for loving reunion between Cordelia and Lear does come, but there are no happy endings in *King Lear*. The desire to stem the tide of suffering in this all-encompassing tragedy led Nahum Tate to give it a happy ending in 1681 – Lear lives, Cordelia and Edgar marry. Tate's version played until 1838 before Shakespeare's original was revived.

Lynn Robson

LAW

the 30-second play

Critics are divided on whether

the playwright had an ordinary or specialized knowledge of law. However, at times he does demonstrate remarkable insights into legal matters. In *Hamlet* the Gravedigger questions the Christian burial of Ophelia when she has drowned herself; at the time a suicide could not be buried in sanctified ground. The Gravedigger debates this; did Ophelia go into the water, or did the water come to her, for if it is the latter she did not drown herself. His debate wittily echoes the actual legal case of Hales v. Pettit, heard in 1560; it is specialist knowledge. Better known is the demand by Shylock in *The Merchant of Venice* for payment of his bond with a pound of Antonio's flesh. This is granted, providing he does not spill a drop of Antonio's blood. It may be just a verbal quibble, but it saves Antonio's life. In *Measure for Measure* the misnamed Angelo makes an outrageous offer – if Isabella, about to become a nun, will sleep with him, he will permit her brother Claudio to live. This is an abuse of Angelo's authority and the law, and he rightly pays for it. 'Let's kill all the lawyers' says Dick the Butcher in *Henry VI Part Two* – but for Shakespeare the law and its terminology were integral to his plays.

RELATED TOPICS
See also
HAMLET
page 22

FALSE ACCUSATION
page 42

3-SECOND BIOGRAPHY
EDMOND MALONE
1741–1812
Major Irish Shakespearean scholar and editor

30-SECOND TEXT
Margrethe Jolly

3-SECOND PROMPT
Shakespeare draws effortlessly upon legal phrases, persons representing the law, and even trial scenes for comic, moral and dramatic purposes.

3-MINUTE CALL
Edmond Malone wondered whether Shakespeare was a lawyer's clerk, though no one has found evidence to support this. Certainly William Shakespeare's life was litigious at times, for he brought actions for debt in Stratford and was a witness in a case in London. But the author's interest in law in the plays was mainly theatrical, as in *The Winter's Tale* when Queen Hermione is tried for adultery and movingly conducts her own defence.

William Shakespeare appreciated the drama of the law court, as in the trial scene in **The Merchant of Venice.**

HISTORY

the 30-second play

RELATED TOPICS
See also
POLITICAL TRANSITION
page 38

USURPATION
page 40

3-SECOND BIOGRAPHIES
EDWARD HALLE
1497–1547
Lawyer and historian

RAPHAEL HOLINSHED
1529–1580
Chronicler of English history

30-SECOND TEXT
Lee Joseph Rooney

3-SECOND PROMPT
Shakespeare's English history plays borrow their source material from the chronicles, but he was always a dramatist first and a historian second.

3-MINUTE CALL
In the early 20th century, some critics claimed that Shakespeare's English histories propagate the 'Tudor myth' – the belief that Henry Tudor was divinely ordained to become king, uniting the warring houses of Lancaster and York and bringing peace to England. However, since then, others have challenged the 'Tudor myth' hypothesis. Indeed, some have even argued that the world that Shakespeare's English histories depict is not explicitly providential at all, but rather subject to the machinations of the scheming and dissembling politicians who inhabit it.

Over the course of his career, Shakespeare is thought to have written and co-written no less than ten English history plays. His main sources were most likely the chronicles of Raphael Holinshed and Edward Halle, but he regularly took liberties with his material, conflating historical personages, collapsing years into mere minutes, and even bringing the dead back to life. Though Joan of Arc was only ten years old when Henry V died, Shakespeare has his death coincide with her rise, as power shifts between England and France in *Henry VI Part One*. In *Henry IV Part One*, though 22 years older, Harry Percy (or 'Hotspur') is made the same age as Prince Hal, for whom he provides a rival and means of redemption in the eyes of the King. Indeed, Hotspur's death by Hal's sword – an invention of Shakespeare's – acts as a symbol of the Prince's reformation from prodigal son to future king. For Shakespeare, hard historical 'fact', if there were even such a thing in 16th-century England, regularly took a backseat to entertaining drama: Richard III is even more bloodthirsty in *Richard III* than in the chronicles, transforming him into a memorable and surprisingly engaging villain. Yet, throughout his histories, Shakespeare's concerns remain the same: the nature of kingship, the changeability of fortune and the forces that drive history itself.

Shakespeare used historical events and people for material, but he didn't always stick to the facts.

GEOGRAPHY

the 30-second play

Although William Shakespeare is not known to have left England, the plays show a fascination with foreign geography and occasionally what sounds like first-hand knowledge. Most of the play settings are from the original stories, but within these settings Shakespeare's imagination roamed from Barbary, Algiers and Alexandria over to 'the vasty wilds of Arabia', on to Damascus, Aleppo and Ephesus. Othello compares his anger 'to the Pontic sea' with a power that 'keeps due on / To the Propontic and the Hellespont'. Shakespeare goes to Corinth, Macedonia and the Peloponnesus, up to Iceland and down to the Antipodes, with numerous references to France, Italy, Spain, Germany and Bohemia. Shakespeare even mentions America and Mexico. By far the most references are to Britain with more than a third of the canon covering English history through the wars, ancient British tales *King Lear*, *Cymbeline*, *Macbeth*, and the contemporary *The Merry Wives of Windsor*. Even when setting a play in a country such as Italy, Shakespeare often uses local English references, as when Sly in *The Taming of the Shrew* claims he is from Burton-heath (Barton on the Heath) in Warwickshire, and Salarino in *The Merchant of Venice* refers to the Goodwin Sands in Kent.

3-SECOND PROMPT
Illustrated books of world cities, travellers' accounts, dramatic maps, active exploration—all stoked Shakespeare's imagination.

3-MINUTE CALL
Queen Elizabeth I arranged travel and trade with the Sultan of Turkey and signed a charter for the Turkey Company of Merchants (Levant Company) to regulate it. Plays about Turks were produced, and travellers wrote exciting accounts of the East. Englishmen stayed in Constantinople and 'turned Turk', while Turkish visitors were not uncommon in London. Perhaps we should not wonder that Shakespeare references this part of the world 100 times.

RELATED TOPICS
See also
LANGUAGE &VOCABULARY
page 58

3-SECOND BIOGRAPHIES
SIR JOHN MANDEVILLE
fl. c.1357
Supposed English traveller to the East

EDWARD BARTON
1562–1598
English ambassador in Constantinople

30-SECOND TEXT
Robin Williams

Even if he never went abroad himself, Shakespeare would have found inspiration in travellers' accounts.

ART

the 30-second play

Where did Shakespeare get his

knowledge of Italian Renaissance art? In the introduction of *The Taming of the Shrew*, Christopher Sly, a tinker tricked into thinking he is a Lord, is promised three 'wanton' pictures: 'Adonis painted by a running brook / And Cytherea [Venus] all in sedges hid'; the maiden Io 'beguiled and surprised'; and Daphne 'roaming through a thorny wood, scratching her legs' with Apollo weeping at her injuries. The sources of Shakespeare's descriptions are not literary: Ovid's Venus is at no point hidden near a brook; his Io is violently raped; his Daphne's legs do not bleed, and his Apollo does not weep. In fact, the first two paintings have been identified as *Venus and the Rose* by Luca Penni and *Io* by Correggio. The narrative of *The Rape of Lucrece* is interrupted in the middle of the heroine's raw grief by a seemingly unnecessary 200 lines describing a vast and complex painting of the Trojan wars, right down to detailed facial expressions; it is not clear why. Shakespeare mentions only one artist by name: 'that rare Italian master' Giulio Romano supposedly made the statue of Hermione in *The Winter's Tale*. Known for his paintings, scholars once thought Shakespeare had erred in making Romano a sculptor, but in fact he was correct.

RELATED TOPICS
See also
CLASSICAL INFLUENCES
page 24

GEOGRAPHY
page 70

3-SECOND PROMPT
Shakespeare let his passion for Italian Renaissance art destroy the structure of one of his poems but where he gained his knowledge is a mystery.

3-MINUTE CALL
Shakespeare delighted in art that was lifelike. Hermione's statue was so skillfully rendered that 'one would speak to her and stand in hope of an answer.' In *Cymbeline*, Iachimo says of the decorations in Imogen's bedroom 'Never saw I figures / so likely to report themselves.' In *Lucrece*'s depiction of Troy, 'many a dry drop seem'd a weeping tear' and 'red blood reek'd'. Shakespeare celebrated art's ability to take us in.

3-SECOND BIOGRAPHIES
ANTONIO ALLEGRI
DA CORREGIO
1489–1534
Painter

GIULIO ROMANO
1499–1546
Painter, sculptor and architect

LUCA PENNI
1500–1556
Painter

30-SECOND TEXT
Ros Barber

Shakespeare was familiar with Italian Renaissance art, such as Corregio's Io.

COMPONENTS

anapest A measure of metrical poetry with the syllable stress pattern weak-weak-STRONG.

blank verse Verse that is written in a regular meter (a fixed rhythmical pattern) but doesn't rhyme. Blank verse is usually written in lines of iambic pentameter, where the syllable pattern weak-STRONG occurs five times per line. Blank verse is different from free verse, which has no rhyme or fixed rhythm.

cittern A metal-stringed instrument from the Renaissance, used for casual music-making, much like a guitar today.

company A playing company was the Elizabethan term for a group of actors who put on plays and performed together.

couplet Two consecutive lines of verse that rhyme with each other.

feet Metrical units used to measure a line of verse, either two or three syllables long. Feet have different names depending on the pattern of rhythmic stress. An iambic foot has the pattern weak-STRONG.

free verse Verse without a regular pattern of rhythm or rhyme.

groundling Those who paid a penny to enter the theatre but not the extra penny for a seat. The groundlings would stand in the yard in front of the stage for the whole performance.

iambic pentameter A line consisting of five metrical units (called 'feet'), at least three of which are 'iambs' (a weak-STRONG syllable pattern). Completely regular iambic pentameter has the rhythm weak-STRONG five times: i-AM-i-AM-i-AM-i-AM-i-AM.

innuendo An insinuation about a person or thing, usually derogatory or suggestive.

lute A stringed instrument with a pear-shaped body and long neck, played by plucking, commonly used in medieval secular music and popular in the Renaissance.

metaphor A figure of speech in which one thing is compared directly to another by saying it is that thing, e.g. 'life is but a walking shadow'.

meter In poetry, the arrangement of words into a regular rhythmical pattern, particularly through the stress pattern of their syllables.

prose Written or spoken language in its ordinary form, without any poetic structure (e.g. meter) imposed upon it. That sentence was prose.

rhyme Rhyme is where two words sound very similar to each other. True rhyme is where two words have identical vowel sounds and end with the same consonant sound, e.g. moon and June. It doesn't matter how they are spelled, only how they sound.

rude mechanicals The six characters in *A Midsummer Night's Dream* who act out the play-within-a-play of *Pyramus and Thisbe*. Their name comes from the fact that they are all manual labourers.

satire A type of comedy that uses irony, exaggeration and ridicule to expose and criticize the behaviour of individuals. Usually topical and often used as a means of undermining those in power.

simile A figure of speech in which one thing is compared directly to another by saying it is like that thing, e.g. 'age like winter bare'.

soliloquy In drama, a short speech spoken by an actor that is overheard by no-one except the audience.

stanza In poetry, another name for a verse. Where some people would say 'this poem has six verses' a poet would say 'this poem has six stanzas'.

swain A young lover or suitor, usually a country youth.

tabor A small drum usually beaten to accompany a pipe or fife played by the same person.

tetrameter A line consisting of four metrical units, or 'feet', which are all identical in their rhythmic pattern.

trochee A measure of metrical poetry with the syllable stress pattern STRONG-weak.

BLANK VERSE

the 30-second play

Three-quarters of Shakespeare's

play text is written in blank verse. Although commonly confused with free verse, blank verse has a regular pattern of rhythm, or meter. It is 'blank' because it has no rhyme at the end of the line. The standard meter of blank verse is iambic pentameter; a line consisting of five metrical units (called 'feet'), most of which are 'iambs' (a weak-STRONG syllable pattern). Therefore most lines in Shakespeare's plays have ten syllables. But iambic pentameter is flexible: up to two of the feet can be substituted with other stress patterns (such as an anapest, weak-weak-STRONG, or a trochee, STRONG-weak). When a line has what is called a 'feminine' ending, an unstressed syllable may be added to it. Some of Shakespeare's most famous and powerful lines vary the blank verse line: to BE / or NOT / to BE / THAT is / the QUES/tion. Blank verse comes close to the natural rhythms of English speech, allowing it to sound less mannered than rhymed verse. But a line-length that is one unit longer than common time (4/4) and the tetrameter sing-song of nursery rhymes, combined with the relative regularity of alternating stresses, elevates the language. Key speeches and soliloquies are written in blank verse, even Caliban's complaints in *The Tempest*.

3-SECOND PROMPT
Shakespeare's plays are written mostly in blank verse; iambic pentameter with no rhyme. Blank verse drama was very new; Shakespeare made it extraordinary.

3-MINUTE CALL
Henry Howard, Earl of Surrey, was the first person to write English blank verse, in his translation of the *Aeneid* (c.1540). The first play written in blank verse was *Gorboduc* (1561) by Thomas Norton and Thomas Sackville. Christopher Marlowe was the first English author to make full use of its potential, and made it an accepted verse form for drama (which had previously been rhyme). Shakespeare subsequently took blank verse drama to new heights.

RELATED TOPICS
See also
RHYME
page 80

PROSE
page 82

3-SECOND BIOGRAPHIES
HENRY HOWARD
1516/17–1547
Earl of Surrey, poet

THOMAS NORTON
1532–1584
Lawyer, politician and writer of verse

THOMAS SACKVILLE
1536–1608
Statesman, poet and dramatist

30-SECOND TEXT
Ros Barber

Shakespeare perfected the blank verse form, with its flexible line of stressed and unstressed syllables.

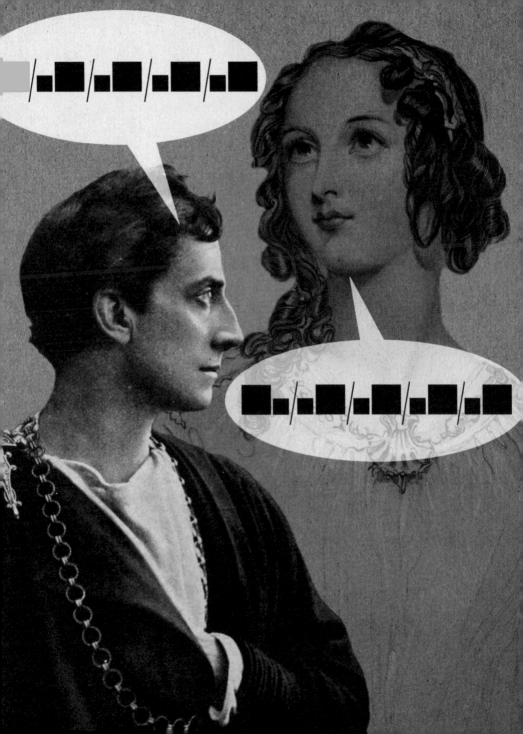

RHYME

the 30-second play

RELATED TOPICS
See also
THE SONNETS
page 28

BLANK VERSE
page 78

PROSE
page 82

3-SECOND BIOGRAPHIES
SIR PHILIP SIDNEY
1554–1586
Poet and courtier

FRANCIS MERES
1565–1647
Author

JOHN MILTON
1608–1674
Poet and author of *Paradise Lost*

3-SECOND PROMPT
Shaping the sound of his poetry and the mood of his scenes, rhyme constitutes an essential component of Shakespeare's work.

3-MINUTE CALL
In Shakespeare's day, rhyme was thought to exert an almost magical power over readers and listeners, delighting them with what Sir Philip Sidney described in his *Defence of Poesy* as 'a certain music to the ear'. For some religiously inclined contemporaries, rhyme's power was understood to be seductive and therefore potentially dangerous; for poets such as John Milton, it was rejected altogether as 'no necessary adjunct or true ornament of... good verse'.

Though the majority of his verse is unrhymed iambic pentameter ('blank verse'), Shakespeare dedicated a significant amount of his energies to rhyme, matching sounds at the end of his verse lines. Indeed, during his lifetime, our bard seems to have been well known for his facility with rhymed verse, his contemporary Francis Meres calling him 'mellifluous & honey-tongued'. Not only are his long narrative poems *Venus and Adonis* and *The Rape of Lucrece* composed entirely of rhymed 'stanzas' (grouped sets of lines), but also 152 of his 154 sonnets share Shakespeare's preferred 'English' rhyme scheme. In his drama, Shakespeare employed rhyme in a number of ways. It both enlivens and brightens the atmosphere of comedies such as *The Comedy of Errors*, *A Midsummer Night's Dream* and *As You Like It*, providing a music of like sounds to bolster the buoyancy. Especially in his early plays, Shakespeare also used rhyme to change the mood of a moment, characters shifting to rhymed language to figure emotional intensity and/or charged interpersonal bonds. Finally, rhyme can commonly be found signalling the conclusions of scenes or long speeches, capping these off with the poetic flourish of a rhymed 'couplet' (two successive rhyming lines).

30-SECOND TEXT
Kirk Melnikoff

Shakespeare mastered the musical qualities of rhyme in both his poems and his plays.

s ne, that over-rul'd, over-sway'd;
ding him Prisoner in a red Rose Chain.
ng temper'd Steel, his stronger Strength obey'd,
was he servile to my coy Disdain.
Oh be not proud, nor brag not of thy Might,
or mastring her, that foil'd the God of Fight!

ch but my Lips with those fair Lips of thine,
(tho' mine be not so fair, yet they are red)
Kiss shall be thine own, as well, as mine.
hat seest thou in the Ground? Hold up thy Head:
ook in mine Eye-balls, where thy Beauty lies,
hen why not Lips on Lips, since Eyes on Eyes?

thou asham'd to kiss? Then wink again,
d I will wink, so shall the Day seem Night,
e keeps his Revels, where there be but twain
bold to play, our Sport is not in Sight.
These blew-vein'd Violets whereon we lean
Never can blab, nor know they what we mean.

e tender Spring, upon thy tempting Lip,
ws thee unripe; yet may'st thou well be tasted,
ke use of Time, let not Advantage slip,
uty within it self would not be wasted.
air Flowers, that are not gather'd in their Prime
ot and consume themselves in little time.

ere I hard favour'd, foul, or wrinkled old,
natur'd, crooked, churlish, harsh in Voice,
er-worn, despised, rheumatick and cold,
ick-sighted, barren, lean, and lacking Juice,
Then mightst thou pause, for then I were not for thee:
But, having no Defects, why dost abhor me?

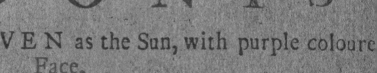

VENUS AND ADONIS.

EVEN as the Sun, with purple coloure
    Face,
    Had ta'n his last Leave of the weepin

    Rose-cheek'd *Adonis* hied him to th
    Chase:
Hunting he lov'd, but Love he laught to
    Sick-thoughted *Venus* makes amain unto him,
    And like a bold-fac'd Suter 'gins to woo him.

PROSE

the 30-second play

Prose, in contrast to blank verse,

is language in its ordinary form without a metrical structure, and gives characters a more natural style of speaking. Shakespeare's prose, however, is often strongly patterned and rhythmical; look at the Porter's speech in *Macbeth*. In the earlier plays, prose is typically used by characters of low status and in comic situations, but the playwright quickly began to develop the use of prose at greater length and in more diverse situations. The importance of prose is often in its situational counterpoint to verse; that is, the shift in language between verse and prose can reveal things about characters and circumstances, especially when someone who typically speaks in verse uses prose. For instance, Lear as a king naturally speaks in verse, but rants in prose when he is losing his mind. In *Julius Caesar*, the speech of the aristocrat Brutus to the citizens is in prose, and Henry V woos Katherine of France in prose. Hamlet meditates on the skull of Yorick in prose. Prose might indicate buffoonery, wit or insanity, as well as a more thoughtful or rational state of mind, of pathos, or simplicity. There is always significance in the shift, and it is a reader's enjoyment to contemplate what that might mean.

3-SECOND PROMPT
When a character speaks in prose instead of verse, Shakespeare is usually telling us something.

3-MINUTE CALL
When watching a performance on stage, it is difficult to tell whether an actor speaks verse or prose. When reading on the page, however, there is a visual clue: the first letter of each line of verse begins with a capital letter, and the lines vary in length. Prose uses sentences that run into each other and generally is typeset into a block paragraph.

RELATED TOPICS
See also
BLANK VERSE
page 78

RHYME
page 80

TURNS OF PHRASE
page 84

30-SECOND TEXT
Robin Williams

Shakespeare used prose for humour, to highlight a character's status or to signal a shift in emotions.

Tam. Let me see. Alas poor *Torick*! I knew him, *Horati*
ellow of infinite Jest; of most excellent fancy,
he hath

born me on his back a thousand times: And how abhorre
my imagination is now, my gorge rifes at it. Here hun
those Lips that I have kifs'd I know not how oft. Whe
be your Gibes now? Your Gambals? Your Songs? Yo
flashes of Merriment that were wont to set the Table on
Roar? No one now to mock your own Jeering? Qui
chop fall'n? Now get you to my Lady's Chamber, and

Enter a Porter.

[*Knocking with*

Port. Here's a Knocking indeed: If a Man were Port
of Hell-Gate, he should have old turning the Key. Knoc
Knock, knock, knock. Who's there, i'th' name of B
zebub ? Here's a Farmer, that hang'd himself on th'e
pectation of Plenty: Come in time, have Napkins enoug
about you, here you'll sweat for't. *Knock.* Knock, knoc
Who's there in th' other Devils Name? Faith, here's
Equivocator, that could swear in both the Scales,
gainst either Scale, who committed Treason enough fo
God's sake, yet could not equivocate to Heaven: Oh com
the Equivocator. Knock, knock, knock. Who

Romans, Country-men, and Lovers, hear me for my
Cause, and be silent, that you may hear. Believe me for
mine Honour, and have respect to mine Honour, that you
may believe. Censure me in your Wisdom, and awake
your Senses, that you may the better judge. If there be
any in this Assembly, any dear Friend of *Cæsar's*, to them
I say, That *Brutus* love to *Cæsar* was no less than his. If
then, that Friend demand, why *Brutus* rose against *Cæsar*,
this is my Answer: Not that I lov'd *Cæsar* less, but that
I lov'd *Rome* more. Had you rather *Cæsar* were living,
and dye all Slaves; than that *Cæsar* were dead, to live all
Free? As *Cæsar* lov'd me, I weep for him; as he was
Fortunate, I rejoyce at it; as he was Valiant, I honour
him: but as he was Ambitious, I slew him. Th

TURNS OF PHRASE

the 30-second play

Shakespeare's memorable

phrases go far beyond those that have been absorbed into the English language as figures of speech. Some are similes: Falstaff says he is as 'melancholy as the drone of a Lincolnshire bagpipe' (*Henry IV Part One*) and *Cymbeline*'s Posthumus, discovering the wife he thought dead is alive, says 'Hang there like fruit, my soul, / Till the tree die.' Other phrases are compressed truths, made powerful through the rhythm of the lines: 'Cowards die many times before their deaths; / The valiant never taste of death but once' (*Julius Caesar*) and Polonius's advice to Laertes: 'This above all; to thine own self be true... Thou canst not then be false to any man.' *Hamlet* is particularly rich with fine turns of phrase: Guildenstern describes a disagreement as 'much throwing about of brains'; Hamlet states 'I am but mad north-north-west. When the wind is southerly, I know a hawk from a handsaw', and, his last words before dying, 'the rest is silence'. He also provides this valuable retort to the cynical: 'There are more things in heaven and earth, Horatio, than are dreamt of in your philosophy.' But beyond quotable quotes, Shakespeare's gift is sheer beauty of expression: 'Light thickens; and the crow / Makes wing to the rooky wood' observes Macbeth; a stab-wound marks 'ruin's wasteful entrance'.

3-SECOND PROMPT
Poetry is memorable language. It is Shakespeare the poet, rather than Shakespeare the playwright, who fills his dramas with compressed and resonant phrases.

3-MINUTE CALL
Memorable imagery is perhaps Shakespeare's greatest gift; and often takes the form of metaphor. Life is 'but a walking shadow' or 'a tale / Told by an idiot, full of sound and fury / Signifying nothing' (*Macbeth*); 'Our doubts are traitors, / And make us lose the good we oft might win / By fearing to attempt' (*Measure for Measure*); 'How sharper than a serpent's tooth it is to have a thankless child' (*King Lear*).

RELATED TOPICS
See also
BLANK VERSE
page 78

RHYME
page 80

THE INVENTOR OF ENGLISH
page 140

30-SECOND TEXT
Ros Barber

Shakespeare had a unique gift for creating vivid and unforgettable phrases.

ROMEO AND JULIET

The tale of star-crossed,

adolescent love, *Romeo and Juliet* is arguably the best-known of Shakespeare's dramas. Few of us have not encountered adaptations in movies, on television, on stage, in novels, in cartoons or in popular music. Fair Verona – be it Shakespeare's Italian burg of the 1400s, the modern metropolis of Luhrmann's 1996 *Romeo + Juliet*, or the post-apocalyptic zombie wasteland of Hollywood's recent *Warm Bodies* – is ubiquitous in the Western world of the 21st century.

Set out in whatever guise, *Romeo and Juliet* appeals to our seemingly universal desire to see love and youthful passion triumph over social obligation. At its start, the play presents a city torn by a longstanding feud between the Montagues and the Capulets, a conflict neither religion nor law can abate. Always unstable, often violent, Shakespeare's Verona is a place of masculine rituals where women subsist as love objects, marital pawns or targets. As the stars and youth would have it, Romeo Montague and Juliet Capulet fall in love at a masquerade ball and, aided by Friar Laurence and the Nurse, the two secretly marry. This happy union, however, is immediately threatened by a deadly skirmish, as Romeo's witty friend Mercutio is killed by Juliet's firebrand cousin Tybalt. When Romeo takes revenge upon Tybalt, he is exiled. In the end, Friar Laurence's attempt to save the day with a 'distilling liquor' goes awry, leaving both young lovers dead, each committing suicide.

Such is the barest outline. Beyond this, what has come to be familiar has only a vague resemblance to what Shakespeare actually wrote. In the popular imagination, Romeo has come to stand for the dreamy swain – sensitive, faithful and poetic – even while Shakespeare gives us a bumbling, fickle protagonist immersed in romantic clichés. Though only 13, Juliet is wiser, more self-aware, and she pines for her Romeo not up on a balcony but at a window. David Garrick's 18th-century ending is still with us as well, reprised in Luhrmann's movie version. There, true love is almost triumphant, Romeo takes the poison seconds before Juliet awakes and dies in her arms. In this, we have a touching tragedy of bad timing instead of Shakespeare's bleak tragedy, his lovers each experiencing death apart and alone in the Capulets' tomb. Cynical as it may be, though, *Romeo and Juliet* is an enticing play of dynamic poetry and compelling characters; it deserves its place as one of Shakespeare's most beloved.

Kirk Melnikoff

MUSIC

the 30-second play

From Bottom's song that wakes

Titania in *A Midsummer Night's Dream* and Desdemona's 'Willow Song' in *Othello*, to Ophelia's 'playing on a lute with her hair down, singing' in *Hamlet*, music is vital to Shakespeare's plays. In addition to songs, Shakespeare often writes about the importance of music and employs musical metaphors: Hamlet, for example, compares himself to the recorder, which Guildenstern cannot play. Songs were often sung by the company clown or fool; Will Kemp played the tabor, and Robert Armin accompanied himself on the cittern for the songs in *Twelfth Night*. Other songs were performed by boys especially trained in singing and lute-playing; for example in *Julius Caesar* where the sweet song of the page Lucius summons up the ghost of Caesar. An Elizabethan audience would have accorded the instruments used in performance with a greater understanding than we do today. Hoboys (shawms, early oboes) were loud instruments often associated with malevolence and frequently presage doom; thus 'the music of the hoboys is under the stage' the night before the battle of Actium in *Antony and Cleopatra*. Trumpet calls were known to those audience members who had fought in wars and had learned what these calls meant in the field. Recorders signified death and the supernatural.

RELATED TOPICS
See also
CONTEMPORARY INFLUENCES
page 26

RHYME
page 80

CLOWNS & FOOLS
page 110

3-SECOND BIOGRAPHIES
THOMAS MORLEY
1557–1602
Wrote music for *As You Like It* and *Twelfth Night*

ROBERT JOHNSON,
1583–1634
Wrote music for *The Tempest*

JOHN WILSON
1597–1674
Wrote music for *Measure for Measure*

30-SECOND TEXT
Claire van Kampen

Clowns and boy performers provided lively musical accompaniment to the plays.

3-SECOND PROMPT
Music is an integral part of Shakespeare's plays, powerfully affecting the atmosphere of particular scenes, with songs functioning in performance as important set pieces.

3-MINUTE CALL
Songs enable characters to express thoughts and emotions they are unable to articulate with words alone. Songs and music also define character status: the earthy Feste ('when that I was and a little tiny boy') whom Shakespeare identifies with the Globe's groundlings, or the innocent Desdemona ('the poor soul sat sighing'), a woman of high grace. Different accompanying instruments are used to support, depict and define the status of the characters to the audience.

COMEDY

the 30-second play

Unlike his contemporaries, Ben Jonson, Thomas Dekker and Thomas Middleton, Shakespeare did not write satirical comedies on London life. Instead, most of his comedies revolve around problems standing between couples and their marriages, but his comedy is varied and versatile. In *The Taming of the Shrew* and *Much Ado About Nothing* subtle wit and innuendo can be found in the banter between Petruchio and Kate, and Beatrice and Benedick. Petruchio's inappropriate wedding costume and the appearance of Bottom as an ass in *A Midsummer Night's Dream* offer visual comedy. The mistaken identities of twins in *The Comedy of Errors*, and the gender-related jokes of cross-dressed heroines in *Twelfth Night* and *As You Like It* allow audiences to laugh at characters' confusions through their own superior knowledge. Lower-class comic characters such as *Much Ado About Nothing*'s Dogberry and *A Midsummer Night's Dream*'s 'rude mechanicals' have lasting appeal in their mangled speeches and endearing foolishness. Shakespeare does not confine his comic flair to comedies, however. The tall tales of Falstaff provoke laughter in the *Henry IV* plays, and his tragedies include some comic scenes: the sardonic Porter in *Macbeth* and the Gravedigger in *Hamlet* offer alternative perspectives on the main action.

RELATED TOPICS
See also
MISTAKEN IDENTITY
page 48

CLOWNS & FOOLS
page 110

THE COMMONERS
page 112

A MIDSUMMER NIGHT'S DREAM
page 126

3-SECOND PROMPT
Master of wit and king of confusions, Shakespeare offers something for everyone in the broad ranging focus and shifting tone of his comedy.

3-MINUTE CALL
Alongside his flair for the comic, Shakespeare is also aware that comedy can be cruel. The binding and imprisonment of Malvolio in *Twelfth Night* is often, in modern productions, played as a nightmare scenario rather than a comic moment. The dispossessing of Jewish Shylock at the end of *The Merchant of Venice* and the 'taming' of Kate in *The Taming of the Shrew* might also play differently to modern sensibilities than to Shakespeare's original audiences.

3-SECOND BIOGRAPHIES
BEN JONSON
1572–1637
Playwright

THOMAS DEKKER
c.1572–1631
Playwright

THOMAS MIDDLETON
1580–1627
Playwright

30-SECOND TEXT
Jessica Dyson

Shakespeare created a range of comic characters, such as Falstaff, Bottom, and the 'rude mechanicals'.

SOLILOQUIES

the 30-second play

3-SECOND PROMPT

Shakespeare's soliloquies are distinctive and subtle compared to those of his contemporaries, creating a window into the minds – and souls – of his tragic characters.

3-MINUTE CALL

Nowhere does Shakespeare use soliloquies more powerfully than in Hamlet, where the Prince of Denmark's private anguish is played out before us in a series of seven soliloquies, conveying the complexities of his inner state. Without them, Hamlet would not have become the iconic character he is, and arguably the play would barely work, since the soliloquies help us understand his otherwise inexplicable behaviour; making him transparent when to all other characters he is opaque.

A dramatic device where a character talks to themselves, unheard by anyone but the audience, most soliloquies before Shakespeare were unsubtle, being used for plot exposition, to reveal plans or to introduce characters. Presaged only by Doctor Faustus's soul-searching soliloquy at the end of Marlowe's play, Shakespeare took soliloquies into new territory, making them powerful psychological explorations of a character's inner state. His soliloquies allow the audience a far more 'interior' experience than drama usually encompasses. Because of the powerful emotional content, it is his soliloquies that are perhaps best remembered and best known, and their ability to engage the audience (with such an intimate sense of a common and flawed humanity) partially explains the enduring popularity of his tragedies. Shakespeare's first foray into the compelling interior drama of a person's mind was *Julius Caesar*'s Brutus; the honest man wrestling with his conscience. Soliloquies reveal not only the tragic hero's dilemmas but also his level of self-awareness or self-delusion; think Macbeth, Othello or Antony. Written in a muscular and flexible blank verse, and vivid with imagery, Shakespeare employed the soliloquy to show us – as we had perhaps never been shown before – the workings of the human mind.

RELATED TOPICS

See also
CONTEMPORARY INFLUENCES
page 26

BLANK VERSE
page 78

TRAGIC HEROES
page 98

3-SECOND BIOGRAPHIES

SAXO GRAMMATICUS
C.1150–C.1220
Danish historian whose story 'Amleth' in *Gesta Danorum* was a source for *Hamlet*

THOMAS KYD
1558–1594
Possible author of an earlier version of *Hamlet* that has not survived

30-SECOND TEXT

Ros Barber

The soliloquy gives the audience access to a character's inner life.

HEROES & VILLAINS

Agincourt The Battle of Agincourt (25 October, 1415) was a major English victory in the Hundred Years War. The English king, Henry V, led his troops into combat and engaged in hand-to-hand fighting. It took place on St Crispin's Day.

chivalry The medieval code of conduct associated with knighthood.

clown A comic entertainer who creates comedy chiefly through exaggerated antics, perhaps with silly clothing. The Elizabethan clown might typically portray himself as a rustic simpleton.

commoner One of the common people; a person without rank or title.

fool A comic entertainer who creates comedy chiefly through wit and words, though there may also be aspects of physical comedy. Stemming from the tradition of court jesters, fools were sometimes retained in royal or noble households.

Great Chain of Being The Great Chain of Being was a pervasive philosophy that confirmed one's place in the world. Everything is both above and below something else on the metaphoric chain that stretches from hell to heaven.

history play A play that is based on real historical events.

jester A professional joker or fool at a medieval court, who would traditionally wear a cap with bells on and carry a mock scepter.

knave A dishonest or unscrupulous man.

knight A man who served his monarch or lord as a mounted soldier in armour; a cavalier; addressed by the title 'Sir'.

Lady Macbeth The wife of Macbeth, who persuades him to murder and usurp his king, only to go mad when she cannot live with the guilt.

Macbeth A Scottish nobleman, the main character of the tragedy that bears his name, who launches into a murdering spree after three witches tell him he will be King of Scotland.

minstrel A medieval singer or musician, especially one who could sing or recite poetry to a musical accompaniment for the nobility.

regicide The killing of a monarch.

rude mechanicals The six characters in *A Midsummer Night's Dream* who act out the play-within-a-play of *Pyramus and Thisbe*. Their name comes from the fact that they are all manual labourers.

sonnet A poem (usually about love) of 14 lines with a fixed rhyme scheme and regular meter (pattern of rhythm) and a 'volta' (turning point), allowing it to, for example, both ask a question and answer it.

tetralogy A work of four parts (whereas a trilogy is a work of three parts).

upper class The ruling classes. Royalty and nobility.

TRAGIC HEROES

the 30-second play

3-SECOND PROMPT

Shakespeare's tragic heroes are, often, less than heroic. They reveal very human characteristics that lead to their – and others' – downfalls and deaths.

3-MINUTE CALL

Romeo (*Romeo and Juliet*) and Antony (*Antony and Cleopatra*) are also tragic heroes. Impetuous Romeo is a victim of circumstance rather than his own actions. He has become synonymous with young love, despite his tragic death. The more mature Antony chooses passion for Cleopatra over duty to Rome and, believing Cleopatra's false story of her own death, dies in an unheroic half-botched suicide. He is, perhaps, the most – and least – admirable of Shakespeare's tragic heroes.

Shakespeare's tragic heroes are just men. Audiences want them to be more – or better – but they are not. This is why they are tragic; this is why they resonate with audiences through time. King Lear has been a great monarch, but he lets his pride get the better of him and disowns his most loving daughter, Cordelia. Cast out by his other daughters, he realizes his mistake and goes mad. Macbeth, a noble military hero, acts swiftly on the witches' prophecies, murdering a king to fulfill his own – and his wife's – ambitions, and orders other murders to keep the throne. The great military leader Othello trusts dishonest Iago too much and is, some critics argue, too easily led to believe his wife is unfaithful. He loses everything, murdering Desdemona and killing himself. Of Shakespeare's heroes, only Hamlet is slow to act, caught in a moral quandary over vengeance and, perhaps, paralyzed by grief for his dead father. Unlike the others, whom audiences may judge more harshly, Hamlet himself wishes he were a better, more heroic, man than he is, calling himself a 'rogue and peasant slave' over his delay in avenging his father's death. Despite being of great social status, Shakespeare's tragic heroes are remembered primarily for their ordinary human emotions and mistakes.

RELATED TOPICS

See also
HAMLET
page 22

OTHELLO
page 44

KING LEAR
page 64

MACBETH
page 104

3-SECOND BIOGRAPHIES

MARCUS ANTONIUS
80 BCE–30 BCE
Roman politician and general

MACBETH
c.1005–1057
King of Scotland

30-SECOND TEXT

Jessica Dyson

Heroes such as Othello, King Lear and Macbeth are tragic because they cannot meet our heroic expectations.

LOVERS

the 30-second play

Twenty-one of Shakespeare's

plays have plots that depend on lovers and their fates, whether they are tragedies that end in death, like *Romeo and Juliet* and *Othello*, or comedies that end in marriage, like *As You Like It* and *The Tempest*. Lovers defy parents, war and disapproving societies. One hundred and fifty-four sonnets narrate a love triangle between a poet, a beautiful youth and a dark-haired woman. One long poem, *Venus and Adonis*, tells what happens when the goddess of love falls in love with an indifferent young man. Shakespeare's most elusive poem – 'The Phoenix and the Turtle' – is about the ecstatic union of two lovers. Love is everywhere but love distorts vision so lovers see only what they want to see. In *A Midsummer Night's Dream*, Helena loves Demetrius although he spurns her and threatens to rape her. In *All's Well That Ends Well*, another Helena adores the worthless Bertram and tricks him into an unwanted marriage. Cleopatra dreams of an idealized Antony and she's willing to give up a kingdom and her life for her vision. Passionate but foolish lovers, like Bassanio in *The Merchant of Venice* and Proteus in *The Two Gentlemen of Verona*, fail to recognize Portia and Julia when the women disguise themselves as men.

3-SECOND PROMPT
In Shakespeare's plays, love transforms: shrew into obedient wife; adoration into jealousy; woman into man and back again; hatred into love; statue into forgiving wife.

3-MINUTE CALL
Shakespeare's true lovers are equal in wit and eloquence: Beatrice and Benedick, Katherine and Petruchio tease and taunt each other; Romeo and Juliet forge a new language of true love. They challenge contemporary poetic conventions, used by poets like Sir Philip Sidney, where silent, distant women are adored by infatuated men. Equality of wit and cross-dressing (seven women dress as men to secure their lovers) mean these characters always question male and female stereotypes.

RELATED TOPICS
See also
THE SONNETS
page 28

COMEDY
page 90

TRAGIC HEROES
page 98

STRONG WOMEN
page 108

3-SECOND BIOGRAPHIES
SIR PHILIP SIDNEY
1554–1586
Courtier and poet. He wrote the influential sonnet sequence *Astrophil and Stella*.

LADY MARY WROTH
1587–1652
Philip Sidney's niece. The first woman to publish a sonnet sequence, *Pamphilia to Amphilanthus*. She also wrote a romantic comedy, *Love's Victory*.

30-SECOND TEXT
Lynn Robson

Shakespeare's vision of true love in **Romeo and Juliet** *has had an enduring appeal.*

FIGHTERS

the 30-second play

Battles, brawls, duels, rebellions,

and even a wrestling match: fighters battle through Shakespeare's comedies, histories and tragedies from the early, barnstorming *Henry VI* tetralogy, to the chivalric brothers-in-arms in *The Two Noble Kinsmen*. They include the charismatic Henry V urging his troops to victory at Agincourt; regicides Richard III and Macbeth; the noble general Othello; and fiery, valiant, doomed Hotspur. Things go awry when fighters translate lessons learned on the battlefield to civic and domestic spaces. In *Much Ado About Nothing*, soldiers Benedick and Claudio, finding themselves in a time of peace and at a loose end, take up the 'merry war' of courtship; Richard III turns his attention to murder. Othello is a great warrior but an insecure husband. Coriolanus refuses to become a politician, preferring banishment so he can seek out Aufidius, the only opponent he wants to fight. Fabled soldier Antony is torn between Rome's military glories, its deadly political games and his passionate love for Cleopatra. Julius Caesar's fame as a warrior is not enough to save him when the conspirators think he's turned into a tyrant. There are also ordinary soldiers, such as Fluellen, Bates and Williams, resigned but willing to fight out of loyalty rather than for a cause that is not theirs or an abstract concept such as honour.

3-SECOND PROMPT
Under the banner of honour, fighters contend for thrones, power, personal glory, land, love, family and to stay alive. The cost is always counted.

3-MINUTE CALL
Shakespeare creates some memorable warrior women – Joan of Arc, Margaret of Anjou, Hippolyta, Cordelia – as well as those, such as Cleopatra, Volumnia and Beatrice, who wish they could be soldiers. Margaret of Anjou is Shakespeare's only female character to kill someone on stage. Monarchs were expected to protect their people and Elizabeth I evoked her warrior-like spirit when England was threatened by the Spanish Armada in 1588.

RELATED TOPICS
See also
POLITICAL TRANSITION
page 38

USURPATION
page 40

HISTORY
page 68

TRAGIC HEROES
page 98

3-SECOND BIOGRAPHY
QUEEN ELIZABETH I
1533–1603
Queen of England, reigned 1558–1603

30-SECOND TEXT
Lynn Robson

Fighters appear in all the play genres, often as flawed heroes.

MACBETH

In *Julius Caesar*, Shakespeare wrote a scene in which a would-be assassin (Brutus) consults with his wife the night before the murder. A few years later, Shakespeare returned to this resonant image, changing the power dynamic, ratcheting up the dramatic tension and surrounding it with the eerie wilds of medieval Scotland. A war hero and his wife commit regicide to take the throne, and then pile on more crimes as they attempt to hold on to power, defying the supernatural forces that first promised their success and destroying their own relationship in the process. In *Macbeth*, Shakespeare created one of literature's most enduring couples, a rare balance of spousal power driven by a passion that is at least as much for each other as for other ambitions.

Some critics blame Lady Macbeth for stepping outside what is appropriate for a woman, and there is no doubt that she does put aside traditional femininity in pursuit of their mutual goals, but given that the play shows women (such as Lady Macduff) to be powerless victims of male violence, this is perhaps understandable. What is clear is that the murder of Duncan is only the beginning of Macbeth's fall, and he accomplishes everything from that point having shut his wife out of the plotting. Indeed, part of his tragedy is his alienation from his wife, so that his famous words on her death ('Tomorrow and tomorrow and tomorrow . . .') are an abstract and nihilistic musing on the pointlessness of existence, and contain none of the tenderness or sense of loss we might expect.

It is important to remember that the impulse to death and violence, far from being introduced into the play by its title character, is its basic environmental structure. We begin in civil war and we end in it, beheading yet another rebel. We begin with a politically incompetent king on the throne and we end not with Fleance – as the witches seemed to promise – but with Malcolm, an unknown quantity whose longest scene (his 'test' of Macduff) raises more questions than answers about his character. We end with a kind of closure, then, but the core issues of society and kingship are far from resolved so that it is easy to imagine the cycle of violence beginning again.

Andrew James Hartley

PLOTTERS

the 30-second play

3-SECOND PROMPT
Whatever their motives –
revenge, power or
troublemaking –
Shakespeare's plotters
make audiences collude
in their schemes, raising
dramatic tension and
heightening comedy
or tragedy.

3-MINUTE CALL
Although some plotters,
such as Iago, are clearly
indefensible, others are
notable for their moral
ambiguity. The scheme
to embarrass Malvolio
begins as a comic plot
but descends to darker
tones in his binding and
imprisonment. In *The
Tempest*, Caliban claims
'this island's mine' and
plots to take it back.
While his plan to kill his
cruel master, Prospero,
is vicious, his motives
echo Prospero's, inviting
audiences to consider
ideas of right and justice.

Plotters abound in Shakespeare's
plays. Large-scale manipulations, such as
Prospero's plot in *The Tempest* to punish his
usurpers and Iago's scheming to bring down
Othello, or minor plots such as the conspiracy
to embarrass Malvolio (*Twelfth Night*) and
illegitimate Edmund's plan to oust legitimate
Edgar from their father's favour (*King Lear*)
engage audiences and raise tensions throughout
Shakespeare's work. We sympathize with some
plotters, such as Hamlet and Titus Andronicus,
who seek revenge for wrongs. Others, such as
Iago, *Cymbeline*'s Iachimo, and *Much Ado About
Nothing*'s Don John, whose plots have dubious
motivations and serious consequences for falsely
accused women, are condemnable in actions but
admirable in ingenuity. Oberon's misogynist plot
to punish disobedient Titania (*A Midsummer
Night's Dream*) backfires, making him cuckold
to a donkey. Political plotting features widely:
the Macbeths murder Duncan for his throne and
plot against others to keep it; in *Julius Caesar*,
Cassius plots not only to kill Caesar out of
jealousy but also to bring the honourable Brutus
into the conspiracy. The history plays, too,
are full of plots and counterplots to take and
maintain the throne, some of which have
indelibly marked our understanding of history, in
particular regarding the character of Richard III.

RELATED TOPICS
See also
USURPATION
page 40

FALSE ACCUSATION
page 42

OTHELLO
page 44

THE TEMPEST
page 146

3-SECOND BIOGRAPHIES
KING RICHARD III
1452–1485
English king who reigned for
two years

HENRY VII
1457–1509
Defeated Richard III to
become king

30-SECOND TEXT
Jessica Dyson

*The audience is
drawn into the
plotters' schemes as
Shakespeare ratchets
up the tension.*

STRONG WOMEN

the 30-second play

3-SECOND PROMPT
Shakespeare is unusual in his time in portraying women who resolutely challenge the status quo of early modern society.

3-MINUTE CALL
Even morally corrupt women, such as Goneril, Regan and Lady Macbeth, have their own forcefulness. Shakespeare also portrays five women unjustly accused of infidelity by jealous husbands, and four women who, scorned by inconstant lovers, persevere with grace. The strength and quiet virtue of so many of these females made Shakespeare a hero of Victorian women in the early waves of feminism.

Remarkable women fill the Shakespearean plays. Every woman is literate, even the shepherdesses Phoebe in *As You Like It* and Mopsa in *A Winter's Tale*. Twelve women defy their fathers to marry the men they choose. Eight women dress as men in order to achieve their aims, including Imogen in *Cymbeline*, who escapes to the Welsh mountains before joining the Roman army; Rosalind in *As You Like It*, who runs away to the forest and buys property; and Portia, who wins a difficult court case in *The Merchant of Venice*. Mistress Quickly, who appears in four plays, manages (and perhaps owns) a tavern. At least 16 women conspire and publicly expose men's dishonest or foolish deeds. Constance of Bretagne and Eleanor of Aquitaine, 77 years old, lead armies in *King John*. Tamora, Queen of the Goths in *Titus Andronicus*, Queen Margaret in four history plays, Cleopatra and Joan of Arc, all lead armies, as well as Fulvia, never seen in *Antony and Cleopatra* but mentioned 18 times. Paulina in *A Winter's Tale* defies a king and controls his destiny for the following 15 years. The longest scene in *Richard III* has three people on stage – Queen Elizabeth, Queen Margaret and the Duchess of York. Although women have fewer words than men in Shakespeare's plays, they have great power and presence.

RELATED TOPICS
See also
FALSE ACCUSATION
page 42

MAGICIANS & WITCHES
page 120

3-SECOND BIOGRAPHIES
BESS OF HARDWICK
1527–1608
Countess of Shrewsbury; was a land magnate and founder of a dynasty

LADY JANE LUMLEY
1537–1578
Translated Euripides from Greek and Latin at 16 years old

MARY SIDNEY HERBERT
1561–1621
Countess of Pembroke; developed a consequential literary circle

30-SECOND TEXT
Robin Williams

Whether good or evil, Shakespeare's female characters are complex and powerful figures.

CLOWNS & FOOLS

the 30-second play

Throughout his writing career, Shakespeare was influenced by the infectious energy of the professional comic performer. When he first arrived in London, the theatres were dominated by the festive vitality of the Elizabethan clown. Invented by England's first celebrity actor Richard Tarlton, this theatrical mainstay was always a bumbling rustic, and his hilarious missteps, physical humour and improvisations thrilled audiences young and old, rich and poor. By Shakespeare's day, William Kempe had inherited Tarlton's mantle, and it was for him that our bard created characters like the Nurse's servant Peter in *Romeo and Juliet*, Bottom in *A Midsummer Night's Dream* and Dogberry in *Much Ado About Nothing*. For reasons that remain unknown, Kempe left the professional stage at the height of his popularity, within months of Hamlet first instructing the Players to 'let those that play your clowns speak no more than is set down for them.' Kempe's place was immediately filled by Robert Armin, a writer, musician and performer. Part idiot, part jester and part prophet, the stage fool was designed by Shakespeare for Armin, and in *As You Like It*'s Touchstone, *Twelfth Night*'s Feste and *King Lear*'s Fool Shakespeare interspersed penchants for music, wit and truth-telling.

3-SECOND PROMPT
Strongly influenced by his era's comedian culture of rustic buffoonery and wise folly, Shakespeare fashioned his own distinctive dramaturgy of festive clowns and knavish fools.

3-MINUTE CALL
The clown's popularity had much to do with Shakespeare's extra-theatrical routines. Tarlton was beloved for his witty extemporal banter with audience members and Kempe for his dancing at the end of performances. Much of the fool's contemporary appeal came from his ancestors: the court jester and the travelling minstrel. Shakespeare's Anglican audiences would also have recognized in the fool the converse of St Paul's dictum 'the wisdom of this world is foolishness in God's sight.'

RELATED TOPICS
See also
CONTEMPORARY INFLUENCES
page 26

KING LEAR
page 64

COMEDY
page 90

A MIDSUMMER NIGHT'S DREAM
page 126

3-SECOND BIOGRAPHIES
RICHARD TARLTON
d.1588
Writer and performer

ROBERT ARMIN
1563–c.1615
Writer, musician and performer

WILLIAM KEMPE
d. c.1610
Performer

30-SECOND TEXT
Kirk Melnikoff

Shakespeare's clowns have their roots in traditional court jesters and minstrels.

THE COMMONERS

the 30-second play

The majority of characters in the plays belong to the upper class. When Shakespeare introduces commoners, the scenes routinely expose subtle yet provocative reflections on their supposed social superiors. Shakespeare rarely limits lower-class characters to mere comic relief; rather, in their often caustic wit they typically reflect on disorder and disunity. The petty squabbles of the nobles are manifested in the petty squabbles of the commoners; duplicity and blind ambition in the upper class is revealed in the actions of those beneath them. Both *Coriolanus* and *Julius Caesar* open with commoners disrupting the order, foreshadowing the actions of the elite. The 'rude mechanicals' of *A Midsummer Night's Dream* provide commentaries on love, not only through the affection of Titania for Bottom, but also in the performance of a disastrous relationship for the royal wedding party. Within a scene of contentious royals in *Henry VI Part Two*, the townsman Simpcox and his wife are exposed as frauds, providing a muted commentary on the court. We also see the deposed Richard II contemplate being a pilgrim, and the fugitive Henry VI desiring the simple life of a shepherd. In Shakespeare's constant exploration of power and society, the commoners play a vital balancing role.

3-SECOND PROMPT

Shakespeare's detailed, sympathetic and humorous depictions of 'commoners' tend to stress, above all, our common humanity.

3-MINUTE CALL

The Great Chain of Being was a pervasive philosophy that confirmed one's place in the world. Everything is both above and below something else on the metaphoric chain that stretches from hell to heaven. A garnet is beneath a diamond on the Great Chain, and a rabbit beneath a lion. So too with humankind: a tailor is beneath a knight who is beneath an earl who is beneath a king.

RELATED TOPICS

See also
PROSE
page 82

COMEDY
page 90

CLOWNS & FOOLS
page 110

3-SECOND BIOGRAPHY

ARISTOTLE
384–322 BCE
Greek philosopher whose theory of *scala naturae* was the basis of The Great Chain of Being

30-SECOND TEXT

Robin Williams

Shakespeare used lower-class characters to mirror and comment on the lives of the elite.

alchemy An early chemistry concerned with trying to convert substances into one another, with a particular focus on turning base metals into gold or a life-giving elixir.

allusion A story or poem with a meaning that can be applied more generally to reveal truths about human existence or which tells another story in a veiled form.

apothecary A person who sells potions, tinctures and herbal remedies; in modern terms, a pharmacist.

Attic The Greek dialect of Attica, the spoken and written language of Athens, in which most ancient Greek literature was written.

Demetrius One of the Athenian lovers in *A Midsummer Night's Dream*.

elixir A magical or medicinal potion.

fairy A mischievous mythical being with miniature human form, originally arising in Celtic and English folklore.

Hermia One of the Athenian lovers in *A Midsummer Night's Dream*. She loves Lysander but is loved by Demetrius.

Hippolyta Amazonian Queen who marries Duke Theseus in *A Midsummer Night's Dream*. A strong woman who does not defer to her husband.

hobgoblin A small, friendly but troublesome mythical being from English mythology. A goblin of the hearth, or 'hob', he might do small jobs around the house if left small gifts, but might just as easily do something wicked. Puck in *A Midsummer Night's Dream* is referred to as a hobgoblin: 'Those that Hob-goblin call you, and sweet Puck, / You do their work, and they shall have good luck.'

metaphor A figure of speech in which one thing is compared directly to another by saying it is that thing e.g., 'life is but a walking shadow'.

Oberon King of the fairies, husband of Titania (*A Midsummer Night's Dream*). To revenge himself on Titania, who has refused to hand over to him her Indian changeling, he instructs Puck to put a special potion on her eyes while she sleeps, so that she will fall in love with the first thing she sees.

philter A magical potion supposed to induce love or desire for a particular person.

Purgatory In Catholic doctrine, a place or state of suffering inhabited by the souls of sinners who must make amends for their sins before they can go to Heaven.

sprite An elusive mythical being. Oberon describes Puck as his 'shrewd and knavish sprite'. Ariel in *The Tempest* is also a sprite.

Theseus Duke Theseus is the ruler of Athens in *A Midsummer Night's Dream*. He and his bride Hippolyta appear only at the beginning and the end of the play.

Titania Queen of the fairies, wife of Oberon (*A Midsummer Night's Dream*). Bewitched by the potion Puck has put on her eyes, she falls in love with Nick Bottom, a weaver and amateur actor whose head has been transformed into a donkey's.

ELIZABETHAN MAGIC

the 30-second play

3-SECOND PROMPT
Magical thinking was normal to Elizabethans. Was there never any such thing as magic, or have we simply lost touch with it?

3-MINUTE CALL
Some claim that without the 'magic' of the Catholic church – its healings, exorcisms, confessions, sacraments, and magical objects imbued with the power of God to protect the wearer – the Elizabethan Protestants had to look elsewhere for their metaphysical sustenance. It did not seem to matter whether the prayer or the charm was actually efficacious – what mattered was the comfort of belief in something ritualistic, which magic could provide.

Magic of many sorts was omnipresent in Elizabethan England. The ancient magical and alchemical writings of Hermes Trismegistus were fashionable. The Earl of Northumberland, the 'Wizard Earl', experimented in the occult, while Simon Forman was employed by nobles for his magical philters and other remedies. The Countess of Pembroke had her own alchemy laboratory. John Dee was reputed to have been given a secret language by angels and Elizabeth I hoped to acquire a small portion of Sir Edward Kelley's magic tincture to raise the money to pay her navy. No wonder Shakespeare's plays are rife with magic in many forms: Glendower is believed to be a magician in *Henry IV Part One*, Othello claims there is magic in the handkerchief, and of course there is *A Midsummer Night's Dream*. Alchemy was much more than the search for a way of transmuting metal into gold – it was a philosophical tradition that included mystical and symbolic aspects. Romeo visits an apothecary shop to buy poison and notes in detail the alchemical apparatus. In *As You Like It* Shakespeare writes a complex alchemical metaphor involving an oak tree, a green and gilded wreathed snake, a lioness and blood, as two brothers transfigure their relationship between the hours of twelve and two. We think of magic as illusion, but it was real to the Elizabethans.

RELATED TOPICS
See also
MAGICIANS & WITCHES
page 120

SPRITES & FAIRIES
page 124

CHARMS & POTIONS
page 130

3-SECOND BIOGRAPHIES
JOHN DEE
1527–1609
Occultist, astronomer, astrologer and mathematician

SIMON FORMAN
1552–1611
Astrologer, occultist and medical practitioner

HENRY PERCY
1564–1632
9th Earl of Northumberland, the 'Wizard Earl'

30-SECOND TEXT
Robin Williams

Alchemy was a popular pursuit in Shakespeare's time, and his work contains numerous references to it.

MAGICIANS & WITCHES

the 30-second play

Theatre – with all its ritual, spectacle and power to move – can feel close to magical. Shakespeare's plays often exploit this dynamic with stories involving people who draw on supernatural abilities for good and evil. Early in his career he wrote Joan of Arc into *Henry VI Part One*, with her mystical power viewed as saintliness by the French and evidence of involvement with black magic by the English. Witchcraft is central to *Macbeth*, providing a major engine of the plot as three 'weird sisters' share half-truths with the title character, which convince him that supernatural forces have made him invulnerable to all who might stand against his bloody rise to power. Late in his career Shakespeare built *The Tempest* around another magician, Prospero, one who uses magic to summon spirits to do his largely benevolent bidding but who also, we later find, has used his power to open graves and communicate with the dead. These plays (like Christopher Marlowe's earlier *Doctor Faustus*, which may have inspired elements of them) make use of stage effects to create a sense of awe, mysticism and excitement, but also exploit audience anxiety that magic might be real, and that the characters are risking their eternal souls.

RELATED TOPICS
See also
MEDICINE
page 62

MACBETH
page 104

ELIZABETHAN MAGIC
page 118

THE TEMPEST
page 146

3-SECOND PROMPT
Despite his genius for character and social politics, Shakespeare and his audience loved the sensational, outlandish and gloriously unreal world of magic.

3-MINUTE CALL
Much of the magic someone such as Prospero uses hinges on illusion, so it is not surprising that these magical effects are often discussed (both in the plays themselves and by subsequent critics) as being metaphors for the art of the theatre, where worlds are created and populated with nothing more than words. As such, Shakespeare himself becomes the master magician, the plays – he seems to suggest – being simultaneously both all powerful and, finally, worthless.

3-SECOND BIOGRAPHIES
JOHN DEE
1527–c.1608
Occultist and mathematician

CHRISTOPHER MARLOWE
1564–1593
Dramatist

30-SECOND TEXT
Andrew James Hartley

As a magician of the stage, Shakespeare created magical characters to enthral his audience.

GHOSTS

the 30-second play

The ghosts in Shakespeare's tragedies, *Hamlet*, *Macbeth* and *Julius Caesar*, and in his histories, *Henry VI* and *Richard III*, are modelled on the avenging and prophetic ghosts of the classical dramas of Aeschylus and Seneca. While Plato disparaged the stage ghosts of Attic tragedies, he nonetheless expounded on the idea that the souls of slain men often pursue their murderers. King Hamlet's ghost demands revenge for his untimely murder, and describes a tormented existence much like a pagan underworld. Banquo's ghost horrifies Macbeth during a banquet, and later frustrates the usurper's ambition to father royalty when the three Weird Sisters ritually invoke the appearance of eight apparitions of future kings of Scotland, descended from Banquo. Shakespeare's tragic ghosts provide far more than sinister dramatic spectacle, but are vital to the plots and represent a supernatural manifestation of divine justice following royal assassination. However, in the romance *Cymbeline*, the ghosts of Posthumus's parents and brothers, who died heroically in battle, enter to offer blessings and call forth Jupiter's protection of Posthumus, and in *The Winter's Tale* Queen Hermione's dream ghost appeals to Antigonus in a way that preserves the infant Perdita.

RELATED TOPICS
See also
CLASSICAL INFLUENCES
page 24

MAGICIANS & WITCHES
page 120

PROPHECY & PREMONITIONS
page 132

3-SECOND BIOGRAPHIES
REGINALD SCOTT
1538–1599
Author of *The Discoverie of Witchcraft*

TIMOTHIE BRIGHT
1551–1615
Author of *A Treatise of Melancholy*

KING JAMES VI OF SCOTLAND
1564–1625
Author of *Daemonologie*

30-SECOND TEXT
Earl Showerman

3-SECOND PROMPT
Shakespeare employed revenge ghosts as instruments of dark prophesy and divine retribution against assassins in both his tragedies and histories. In his romances, however, Shakespeare's ghosts are depicted as benevolent influences.

3-MINUTE CALL
In the 16th century, ghosts were variously believed to be demons, portentous evil spirits or the souls of the deceased undergoing a period of purification as in the Catholic Purgatory. Sceptics considered ghosts to be hallucinations or delusions. Whatever Shakespeare's audience believed about ghosts, these dramatized spirits came to inhabit the imaginative void left open by the banishment of Purgatory under English Protestantism in 1563.

Following the classical tradition, Shakespeare's ghosts are vengeful and prophetic spirits.

SPRITES & FAIRIES

the 30-second play

3-SECOND PROMPT
For Shakespeare, sprites and fairies don't just make plots work, they hint at everything in the world that is beyond human control and understanding.

3-MINUTE CALL
The fairy imagined by Mercutio and those of *A Midsummer Night's Dream*, are tiny creatures who travel in coaches made of hazelnut shells, sleep in snake skins, and hunt bees, but they have intimate relationships with people. It's not entirely clear how the physics of this works – sometimes fairies seem the same size as people, and sometimes they seem to have shrunk humans to their scale – but Shakespeare never let logistics stand in the way of a good story.

However well-read, and whatever command he had of international and historical cultures, Shakespeare was fascinated by a distinctly English and rural folk tradition. It appears frequently in allusion and metaphor, as when Mercutio in *Romeo and Juliet* speaks at length about a dream-bringing fairy called Queen Mab, but Shakespeare brings such creatures literally onto the stage in *A Midsummer Night's Dream* and, in a slightly different form, in *The Tempest*. In the latter play, Ariel is a spirit of air, water and fire; a shape shifter; and master of music and illusion. The fairies of the earlier play are rooted in the earth and the woods, and grow more out of the playwright's native English countryside than they do out of the Athenian forest that is their home in the play. They are led by a king and queen, Oberon and Titania, both attended by servant fairies, one of whom – Puck – is a wilful troublemaker who delights in causing chaos. Though his antics largely result in harmless mischief, he is also a 'hobgoblin' capable of nightmarish appearances, and the feuding of the fairies in the play has devastating effects on the weather and landscape. They remind us that for Shakespeare's audience, there was much about the world that they did not understand and of which they had learned to be wary.

RELATED TOPICS
See also
ELIZABETHAN MAGIC
page 118

A MIDSUMMER NIGHT'S DREAM
page 126

THE TEMPEST
page 146

30-SECOND TEXT
Andrew James Hartley

Shakespeare's fairies draw on folk traditions and help to represent the mysteries of life.

A MIDSUMMER NIGHT'S DREAM

This is – some would have us believe – Shakespeare at his most child-friendly: a silly romantic comedy with magic, fairies, a goofy playlet and happy endings all round. This is the play as the Victorians saw it, all flowers and balletic fairies, often played by children. But a closer look at the play shows something altogether darker and more troubling.

We open on the eve of two forced marriages – Theseus to the captured Hippolyta, and, under threat of death if she disobeys, Hermia to Demetrius. The seasons have been turned cataclysmically on their heads by Oberon and Titania's feuding, a struggle nominally about ownership of an Indian boy, but also driven by the sexual jealousy tying the fairies to the humans of the main plot. The stakes are high, and the bitterness of everyone involved (including those sparring couples who wander into the woods) turns the dream into a nightmare, where nothing behaves as it should, where lovers betray each other for no apparent reason, and where the threat of death is real and ever present.

Things seem to resolve happily, but they do so strangely. The opening tension between Theseus and his taciturn bride vanishes without the two being on stage in the interim, but their fairy alter egos (Oberon and Titania) are present throughout the forest section. On Shakespeare's stage most actors would have played more than one role, and it makes psychological sense to see the Theseus/Hippolyta struggle played out through the fairy king and queen who probably looked exactly like them.

All of the play's struggles (even the one in *Pyramus and Thisbe*) are about power, control and desire, and the outcomes are less clear than we might assume. Oberon strips Titania of her will, which is supposedly what he wanted, but in the process he makes himself personally and sexually irrelevant to her, and it is telling that when he removes the charm from her sight his spell asks that she come back not more submissive, but as her old feisty self. The woods allow experimentation with, and reversal of, usual roles, so that those used to being adored are scorned and vice versa, but harmony is finally attained through mutuality, through a balance of power, and those who would insist upon patriarchal authority (such as Hermia's father) are overruled. These are deeper, darker waters than most children can swim in.

Andrew James Hartley

MONSTERS

the 30-second play

Like every society before it and after, Shakespeare's England imagined a world full of monsters. A motley array inciting fear, disgust and fascination, these beings were sometimes conjured, sometimes discovered in the dark wake of assumptions about normalcy and transgression. 'Barbaric' tribesmen – brought back from England's earliest colonial voyages – were offered for penny views at London's fairs, and on the city's bookstalls were to be found tales of fantastic creatures, abominable fiends, deformed personages, and the like. Shakespeare was no stranger to this early modern fascination, his language fraught with various images of the monstrous. Romeo calls death a 'lean abhorred monster'; Macduff promises to see Macbeth punished 'as our rarer monsters are'; and Iago infamously warns Othello to 'beware jealousy / It is the green-eyed monster.' Shakespeare also stages monsters in his plays: the disfigured Richard in *Richard III*; the transfigured Bottom in *A Midsummer Night's Dream*; the unsettling witches in Macbeth; and, son of the "foul witch Sycorax', the disaffected Caliban in *The Tempest*. With their troubling appearances and actions, these characters continue to captivate in their manifestations on film and on stage, encouraging us to recognize monsters not just without but also within.

RELATED TOPICS
See also
A MIDSUMMER NIGHT'S DREAM
page 126

THE TEMPEST
page 146

3-SECOND PROMPT
With his contemporaries, Shakespeare shared a fascination with the monstrous; not only do his plays frequently refer to monsters but some also stage them as well.

3-MINUTE CALL
As the 16th century came to a close, Shakespeare and his contemporaries focused more and more upon the monsters potentially lurking in each and every one of us; these, it was thought, were scarier creatures than those to be encountered in the natural world. Indeed, just as his contemporary Montaigne exposed the barbarity of the civilized in his foundational essay 'Of Cannibals', Shakespeare's alter ego Prospero tellingly concludes of Caliban 'this thing of darkness I acknowledge mine.'

3-SECOND BIOGRAPHY
MICHEL DE MONTAIGNE
1533–1592
Essay writer

30-SECOND TEXT
Kirk Melnikoff

Shakespeare was fascinated by the monstrous 'other' as well as the monster within.

CHARMS & POTIONS

the 30-second play

From *Carduus benedictus*
(holy thistle) to soothe a qualm of the heart
in *Much Ado About Nothing* to the magic
flower that charms the eyes of sleeping lovers
in *A Midsummer Night's Dream*, Shakespeare
includes a variety of poisons, concoctions and
magical charms – real and imagined – throughout
the plays. Both Juliet (*Romeo and Juliet*) and
Imogen (*Cymbeline*) drink an elixir that induces
a deep sleep resembling death. Charms are
blamed when love is perceived as unwarranted,
as Desdemona's father insists when she falls
in love with Othello; Egeus in *A Midsummer
Night's Dream* believes Lysander wooed his
daughter with bewitchments. Shakespeare's
knowledge of herbal lore is impressive. He
understood that herbs need to be gathered at
certain times, depending on their use: 'root of
hemlock, digg'd in the dark' refers to gathering
the plant during the new moon, the appropriate
time to collect the elements necessary to
discover one's Fate, while slips of the poisonous
yew tree are 'sliver'd in the Moon's eclipse', cut
off in shreds during the moon's waning, the
traditional time to collect plants for curses or
banishings. Friar Laurence in *Romeo and Juliet*
gathers herbs in the early dew and confirms that,
'O mickle [much] is the powerful grace that lies /
In herbs, plants, stones, and their true qualities.'

RELATED TOPICS
See also
MEDICINE
page 62

ELIZABETHAN MAGIC
page 118

MAGICIANS & WITCHES
page 120

3-SECOND PROMPT
Shakespeare's work
includes more detailed
information about
charms and potions
than about battles.

3-MINUTE CALL
According to ancient
herbals and cookbooks,
the ingredients in the
cauldron in *Macbeth* are
herbs and plants: eye of
newt is mustard seed;
tongue of dog is a leaf
from the hound's tongue
plant; scale of dragon is a
leaf of dragon-wort,
otherwise known as
tarragon, whose Latin
name means 'little dragon'.
Mummy, a medicament
from dried bodies, was
popular among the
Elizabethans and
was sold in the Merck
pharmaceutical catalogue
until 1908.

3-SECOND BIOGRAPHIES
PARACELSUS
c.1493–1541
Physician, botanist and
astrologer mentioned by
Shakespeare

JOHN GERARD
1545–1612
English herbalist

30-SECOND TEXT
Robin Williams

*Shakespeare had a
detailed knowledge
of herbal lore, as shown
in the witches' spell
in* Macbeth.

PROPHECY & PREMONITION

the 30-second play

Shakespeare's plays abound with

prophecies and premonitions. In *Richard III*, Richard plants a misleading prophecy to incriminate his brother, Clarence, who himself experiences a terrifying nightmare of his own death at sea – a premonition that is soon fulfilled when he is drowned in a barrel of wine by Richard's assassins. In the same play, Margaret's eerily prophetic curses anticipate the deaths of numerous characters (including Richard). In *Troilus and Cressida*, Cassandra predicts the fall of Troy, and, in *Julius Caesar*, Caesar's wife, Calpurnia, dreams that he will die in her arms. Joan la Pucelle of *Henry VI Part One* derives her prophetic powers from an unholy pact with demonic 'fiends', and, in *Henry VI Part Two*, the sleeping Duke of Gloucester experiences a gruesome premonition that seems to foretell his downfall – the ambitious Duchess, however, dreams that she will become queen. Finally, the beguiling (but often confounding) predictions of the three witches entice Macbeth into increasingly shocking acts of violence, even convincing him that 'no man of woman born' can harm him. Ironically, it is revealed that Macbeth's nemesis, Macduff, was born by caesarean, demonstrating the dangers of prophecies.

RELATED TOPICS
See also
BIBLICAL REFERENCES
page 60

MACBETH
page 104

ELIZABETHAN MAGIC
page 118

MAGICIANS & WITCHES
page 120

3-SECOND PROMPT
Shakespeare sometimes uses prophecies to 'signpost' where the story is going, but they just as often worked as riddles for characters – and the audience – to decipher.

3-MINUTE CALL
Although prophecies were generally thought to express the will of God, in Shakespeare's plays their meaning – and even their authenticity – is often ambiguous. Indeed, they are just as likely to create uncertainty as they are to clarify, deceiving characters and audience alike. In the English history plays especially, the problem of interpreting prophecies and premonitions serves as an analogy for the difficulty of making sense of both history and the forces that drive it.

3-SECOND BIOGRAPHIES
HENRY HOWARD
1540–1614
1st Earl of Northampton who wrote against the 'poyson of supposed prophecies'

RICHARD HARVEY
1560–1630
Clergyman who predicted disasters in 1588

WILLIAM HACKETT
d.1591
Self-proclaimed prophet

30-SECOND TEXT
Lee Joseph Rooney

Cassandra predicts the fall of Troy but in other plays, prophecies are not to be trusted.

LEGACY

Anne Hathaway The maiden name of the wife of William Shakespeare.

Ariel A mischievous sprite in *The Tempest*.

attribution The act of ascribing a work to a particular artist or author.

Bardolatry Idolatry with its focus on "The Bard"; the worship of William Shakespeare as though he were a god.

blank verse Verse that is written in a regular meter (a fixed rhythmical pattern) but doesn't rhyme. Blank verse is usually written in lines of iambic pentameter, where the syllable pattern 'weak-STRONG' occurs five times per line. Blank verse is different from free verse, which has no rhyme or fixed rhythm.

Caliban A character in *The Tempest*. A bestial half-man whose mother was the witch Sycorax, and who (somewhat unwillingly) serves Prospero.

collocation In linguistics, the habitual placing of a word with another word or words with a frequency greater than chance.

cultural consciousness An awareness of your own culture, and of how it compares with other cultures.

David Garrick An influential Shakespearean actor and theatre impresario (1717–1779) who was responsible for the first major Shakespeare festival, the Shakespeare Jubilee of 1769. He influenced nearly all aspects of theatrical production in the 18th century.

inkhorn term A word from a foreign language used in English and deemed to be unnecessary or pretentious.

Machiavellian Adhering to the principles outlined by Niccolo Machievelli (1469–1527) in his work *The Prince*, an exploration of how to achieve and hold onto political power, the essence of which is often stated as 'the end justifies the means'. The term Machiavellian is applied to people who are scheming and ruthless in their quest for power.

masque A form of amateur dramatic entertainment popular among the nobility in the 16th and 17th centuries, involving dancing and acting by masked performers.

Prospero The main character of *The Tempest*; the exiled Duke of Milan who, through studying certain books, has become a powerful magician.

Romantic poetry Romanticism was a cultural movement of the mid-to-late 18th century (and very early 19th century) that reacted against the more rational/scientific values of The Enlightenment. Romantic poets included Wordsworth, Keats, Shelley, Byron and Coleridge, who favoured writing about nature, and more personal and emotional subjects.

soliloquy In drama, a short speech spoken by an actor that is overheard by no-one except the audience.

sprite An elusive mythical being. Oberon describes Puck in *A Midsummer Night's Dream* as his 'shrewd and knavish sprite'. Ariel in *The Tempest* is also a sprite.

stage direction An instruction in the text of a play indicating the setting, the position or movement of an actor or actors, the tone of a piece of dialogue or any sound and lighting effects.

THE KING OF INFINITE SPACE

the 30-second play

For all their richness and complexity as the stuff of private reading, Shakespeare's plays are not novels or poems, but scripts, and only attain their intended completion when embodied and spoken by actors. On the page, the plays contain little more than character names and dialogue—even stage directions (frequently added by editors) are used very sparingly – but the text's limited clues to staging open up a wide variety of possibilities. Rather than pursuing a 'correct' staging, therefore, or somehow pointing back to the way the plays were first performed, the text becomes the source material for a new art object collaboratively generated through the interaction of the theatre company with the words of the text. However static the play text, a key element of the final product (the company's membership) is always new, and brings to the work their own concerns and tastes, so the performance history of any Shakespeare play is necessarily and healthily a record of that culture's artistic and political evolution. A good production finds a pressing resonance in the script, something that makes its content immediate, so that the audience is treated not just to a Shakespeare play from the past, but one that speaks to them directly, exploring ideas and issues with which they connect.

RELATED TOPICS
See also
CONTEMPORARY INFLUENCES
page 26

THE STORYTELLER
page 142

3-SECOND BIOGRAPHIES
RICHARD BURBAGE
1567–1619
Actor and theatre owner

DAVID GARRICK
1717–1779
Shakespearean actor and impresario

PETER HALL
1930–
Director and founder of the Royal Shakespeare Company

30-SECOND TEXT
Andrew James Hartley

3-SECOND PROMPT
Shakespeare's text is only a beginning. The play on stage is a living, breathing organism that is never the same twice.

3-MINUTE CALL
A production (or movie) of *Julius Caesar* might be set in first-century Rome, but it might also work set in Nazi Germany, or in present-day London, as an exploration of contemporary politics and media manipulation of the public. Different theatre companies in different time periods find different elements of the play exciting and ripe for exploration, so the play evolves, retaining – when done well – that electrifying freshness it had when it was first staged.

Theatre companies can adapt Shakespeare's plays to suit any culture or time period.

THE INVENTOR OF ENGLISH

the 30-second play

3-SECOND PROMPT
Like most of his contemporaries, Shakespeare delighted in linguistic innovation, and four centuries later, many of his new words and phrases are part of everyday English.

3-MINUTE CALL
Shakespeare's coinages were created in different ways. Sometimes he added affixes to words already in the language, such as 'laughable', 'dislocate' and 'courtship', particularly 'un' in 'unnerved', 'unknowing' and 'unpolluted'. Sometimes he formed hyphenations, such as 'smooth-faced' and 'tongue-tied', a number of which have become today's collocations: 'pell mell', 'fair play' and 'fancy free'. Like his character Armado in *Love's Labour's Lost*, Shakespeare seems to be 'a man of fire-new words'.

Elizabethans argued about new words entering English – were they 'inkhorn' terms to be despised and rejected, or were they necessary to describe new concepts and embellish the language? Shakespeare relished adding words to English. Some have not survived ('exsufflicate' in *Othello*, for example). Shakespeare provides definitions for some: Macbeth laments that his hands are so stained with King Duncan's blood that washing them will turn the 'multitudinous seas incarnadine, / Making the green one red.' Lady Macbeth wants to 'unsex' herself, a word that endures because of the play itself. Others, such as 'accommodation' (*Measure for Measure*) and 'assassination' (*Macbeth*), are commonplace today. More memorable and instantly recognizable are a host of phrases that we use and which are all Shakespeare's. We talk of someone being 'hoist with his own petard', say that 'brevity is the soul of wit', refer to what we see in 'my mind's eye', and use phrases such as 'To be or not to be' and all the punning versions of it, such as 'taboo or not taboo', and 'to the manner born' – all from *Hamlet*. The journalist Bernard Levin drew up a list of more than 50 such phrases: if we say 'It's Greek to me', or it's 'dead as a doornail', or 'vanished into thin air', then, says Levin, we are quoting Shakespeare.

RELATED TOPICS
See also
LANGUAGE & VOCABULARY
page 58

TURNS OF PHRASE
page 84

3-SECOND BIOGRAPHY
BERNARD LEVIN
1928–2004
Journalist, author, and broadcaster

30-SECOND TEXT
Margrethe Jolly

It is estimated that Shakespeare added at least 1,700 words to the English language.

hoist with his own petard

accommodation

my mind's eye

brevity is the soul of wit

unsex

assassination

exsufflicare

THE STORYTELLER

the 30-second play

Like most writers of his day,

Shakespeare borrowed extensively when it came to constructing his plots – from history and mythology, from earlier versions of the same stories, and from what other playwrights were doing. In each case he made the story his own by giving it a twist that would surprise even those who thought they knew what was coming (as when he kills Cordelia in *King Lear*, for instance), by creating new characters, and by writing in a way that transformed the story utterly and made it new. As his prominence increased over time and his stories became central to culture and education, subsequent writers have done something similar, repurposing his plots in the creation of new books and scripts. The plot of *King Lear*, for instance, was rewritten by Jane Smiley as *A Thousand Acres*, a novel about the daughters of an Iowa farmer. Stage musicals such as *West Side Story* and *Kiss Me Kate* are the descendants of *Romeo and Juliet* and *The Taming of the Shrew*, while some creative reimagining turned *Hamlet* into *The Lion King*. Television shows such as *House of Cards* borrow from *Richard III*, not just in representing Machiavellian politics, but also through the central character's method of talking directly to the audience as he takes them into his confidence.

RELATED TOPICS
See also
TEXTUAL SOURCES
page 20

THE KING OF INFINITE SPACE
page 138

3-SECOND BIOGRAPHIES
COLE PORTER
1891–1964
Songwriter and composer

JANE SMILEY
1949–
Novelist

30-SECOND TEXT
Andrew James Hartley

3-SECOND PROMPT
Shakespeare today is not just an author or a collection of known works, but a field of cultural production with its own life and energy.

3-MINUTE CALL
Authors can adapt Shakespeare because the plays are outside copyright protection, but the appeal to writers is more than that. When you retell an old story you tap into a cultural consciousness that reaches back in time, while making something that – if successful – feels compellingly new. You become part of a living narrative tradition, one in which Shakespeare himself participated not simply as an originator but as an adapter of other people's stories.

Romeo and Juliet *has been retold in modern times as the musical* **West Side Story.**

INFLUENCE

the 30-second play

Is Shakespeare more influential than any other writer? How many works of art reference Shakespeare's plays and poems? Shakespeare's influence is global, and reaches all art forms. It is estimated that, among British artists alone, pictures depicting Shakespearean scenes account for about one fifth – around 2,300 – of the total number of recorded literary paintings between 1760 and 1900. In addition to the numerous retellings of his stories under different guises and in different genres, phrases from his plays and poems have become the titles of hundreds of plays, novels, movies and songs. After the Bible, no book – and no single author – is quoted more often than Shakespeare. He strongly influenced the Romantic poets: John Keats kept a bust of The Bard by him when he wrote, producing poems full of Shakespearean imagery, and Samuel Taylor Coleridge was equally inspired, writing numerous influential essays on his work. Charles Dickens was deeply influenced by Shakespeare, quoting him often and using his phrases for at least 25 of his titles. Thomas Hardy and Herman Melville similarly acknowledged Shakespeare's influence; Melville even included stage directions and soliloquies in *Moby Dick*. Shakespeare continues to inspire modern writers, artists, filmmakers, musicians and theatre practitioners.

RELATED TOPICS
See also
TURNS OF PHRASE
page 84

THE STORYTELLER
page 142

CRITICAL HERITAGE
page 152

3-SECOND PROMPT
His gift at turning a phrase, combined with a cultural penetration second only to the Bible, make Shakespeare the most influential writer of all time.

3-MINUTE CALL
Many works owe their titles to Shakespeare, including Agatha Christie's *The Mousetrap*, Alfred Hitchcock's *North by Northwest*, David Foster Wallace's *Infinite Jest* (*Hamlet*), Ray Bradbury's *Something Wicked This Way Comes*, William Faulkner's *The Sound and the Fury* (*Macbeth*), Alistair MacLean's *Where Eagles Dare* (*Richard III*), Thomas Hardy's *Under the Greenwood Tree* (*As You Like It*), Frederick Forsyth's *The Dogs of War* (*Julius Caesar*), Aldous Huxley's *Brave New World* (*The Tempest*) and H.E. Bates's *The Darling Buds of May* (*The Sonnets*).

3-SECOND BIOGRAPHIES
JOHN KEATS
1795–1821
Poet

CHARLES DICKENS
1812–1870
Novelist

HERMAN MELVILLE
1819–1891
Novelist and poet

30-SECOND TEXT
Ros Barber

Shakespeare inspired Coleridge, Melville, Dickens, Keats and Hardy.

THE TEMPEST

Written late in Shakespeare's career, *The Tempest* fittingly begins on a wayward ship amid a powerful storm. What appears to be a natural phenomenon, though, is quickly revealed to be a magical ruse, one conjured by the play's prime-mover as a vehicle of his revenge. Prospero was once Duke of Milan, but at the beginning of the play he subsists as a deposed and exiled patriarch, living on an enchanted island with his daughter Miranda, his native-drudge Caliban, and sprite-servant Ariel. As fate would have it, the skirting ship hails from Milan, and its passengers include Prospero's brother Antonio and Alonso, the King of Naples, both prime movers behind the conjuror's earlier downfall. Subsequently shipwrecked on the island in three parties, this crew is subject in different ways to a Prospero bent on meting out justice and reclaiming his dukedom. Along the way, the play can be understood to explore the limitations of revenge, the power of forgiveness, and the ways and costs of colonial authority. Ultimately, it ends happily, with Prospero reconciled to those who wronged him, including Caliban, and his daughter engaged to Alonso's son Ferdinand.

Like *A Midsummer Night's Dream*, *The Tempest* stands as one of Shakespeare's most self-conscious of endeavours in its focus on art, the artist and the imagination. From its opening storm, to its central masque of gods and reapers and its airy banquet, the play again and again stages art's power to move, to teach and to transform. That, however, is not the whole story. In one of Shakespeare's most memorable speeches, Prospero also comes to admit the inadequacy of his art, recognizing that even 'the great globe itself, / Ye all which it inherit, shall dissolve / And . . . / Leave not a rack behind.' For centuries, Prospero's wistfulness has been taken by some as Shakespeare's own, *The Tempest* as our playwright's farewell to the theatre. That Shakespeare would continue to write plays can be taken either to refute these claims or to suggest a change of heart.

Along with inspiring many faithful renderings on stage, *The Tempest* has also long proven amenable to various forms of alteration. Past centuries have seen a plethora of *Tempest* adaptations, operas, burlesques, spin-offs and musical extravaganzas. More recently, the play has spawned numerous movie adaptations including Fred Wilcox's *Forbidden Planet* (1956), Derek Jarman's *The Tempest* (1979), Peter Greenaway's *Prospero's Books* (1991) and Jim Sheridan's *In America* (2002).

Kirk Melnikoff

APOCRYPHA

the 30-second play

A curious number of plays were published in Shakespeare's lifetime, under his name or initials, which do not appear to have been his. *Locrine* (1595) was published as 'Newly set forth, overseen and corrected by W.S.' *Thomas Lord Cromwell* (1602) and *The Puritan Widow* (1607), were also attributed to 'W.S.' His full name was given as the author of *The London Prodigal* (1605), *A Yorkshire Tragedy* (1608), and *Pericles* (1609). After his death, *Sir John Oldcastle*, originally published anonymously in 1600, was republished under Shakespeare's name in 1619. All of these plays were included in the *Third* and *Fourth Folios* of 1663 and 1685, although now only Pericles is accepted as (at least partially) his. Of the 20 poems published under Shakespeare's name in *The Passionate Pilgrim* (1599 and 1612) only five are his; others are by Thomas Heywood, Richard Barnfield, Christopher Marlowe and Sir Walter Raleigh. Some scholars think Shakespeare may have had a hand in *Edward III* (1596), and that he rewrote part of *Sir Thomas More*. *The Two Noble Kinsmen* was published in 1634 as being by Shakespeare and John Fletcher, an attribution that is generally accepted. Certain scholars have argued that manuscript plays *Thomas of Woodstock* (also known as *Richard II Part One*) and *Edmund Ironside* are Shakespeare's.

3-SECOND PROMPT
The poems and plays of others were published under Shakespeare's name in his lifetime. Modern scholars are still trying to determine the full extent of Shakespeare's canon.

3-MINUTE CALL
Arden of Faversham, an anonymous blank verse play published in 1592, has sometimes been at least partially attributed to Shakespeare and contains characters named Black Will, Shakebag and the Ardens. This combination of names appears to point to William Shakespeare, whose mother's maiden name was Mary Arden. But the play is based on a real murder that took place on 14 February, 1551 in Faversham, Kent, and all these names are real.

RELATED TOPICS
See also
CONTEMPORARY INFLUENCES
page 26

CO-AUTHORSHIP
page 32

CRITICAL HERITAGE
page 152

3-SECOND BIOGRAPHIES
THOMAS HEYWOOD
1570/5–1641
Playwright, poet and actor

RICHARD BARNFIELD
1574–1620
Poet

JOHN FLETCHER
1579–1625
Jacobean playwright

30-SECOND TEXT
Ros Barber

Shakespeare's name was attached to several poems and plays that he did not write.

FORGERIES

the 30-second play

Stratford-upon-Avon resident

Mr Williams liked to amuse himself by telling visitors he had burned a stack of Shakespeare's papers. Told this on a visit to Stratford in 1795, Samuel Ireland exclaimed to his 19-year-old son William Henry, 'I would give half of my precious library for a single example of the great Bard's writing.' Weeks later, the son presented him with a receipt signed by Shakespeare. The paper was 16th century, the ink brown and faded; the father was convinced. More followed. A love letter from Shakespeare to Anne Hathaway. Correspondence with Elizabeth I. A handwritten manuscript of *King Lear*. Notes for *Hamlet*. And a brand new play, *Vortigern and Rowena*. But William Henry Ireland was no Shakespeare. On *Vortigern*'s opening night, Shakespearean scholar Edmund Malone published his report on the Ireland papers, declaring them forgeries. Fifty-seven years later John Payne Collier, a respected Shakespearean scholar, presented an amazing discovery: a *Second Folio* (1632) of Shakespeare's works, covered in thousands of notations that Collier claimed were the author's. Denounced as a forgery eight years later, it was subsequently discovered that Collier had added lines and words to dozens of documents. To this day, scholars are loath to trust anything that passed through Collier's hands.

3-SECOND PROMPT
The disappointing absence of personal papers in Shakespeare's hand, combined with his status as a literary idol, has led to some spectacular forgeries.

3-MINUTE CALL
Did Shakespearean forgery begin with David Garrick's Shakespeare Jubilee of 1769? Shakespeare's house, New Place, was demolished in 1702, and its replacement was also flattened in 1759, but local carvers bought the wood from the garden's mulberry tree, said to have been planted by Shakespeare himself. During Garrick's Jubilee, hundreds of mulberry wood souvenirs were sold; many more than a single tree could provide. Samuel Ireland himself had a mulberry wood goblet.

RELATED TOPICS
See also
THE LIFE & LEGEND
page 16

CRITICAL HERITAGE
page 152

3-SECOND BIOGRAPHIES
DAVID GARRICK
1717–1779
Influential actor, playwright and theatre manager

WILLIAM HENRY IRELAND
1775–1835
Poet and forger

JOHN PAYNE COLLIER
1789–1883
Shakespearean scholar and forger

30-SECOND TEXT
Ros Barber

Shakespeare's legendary status created a market for dubious souvenirs and forgeries.

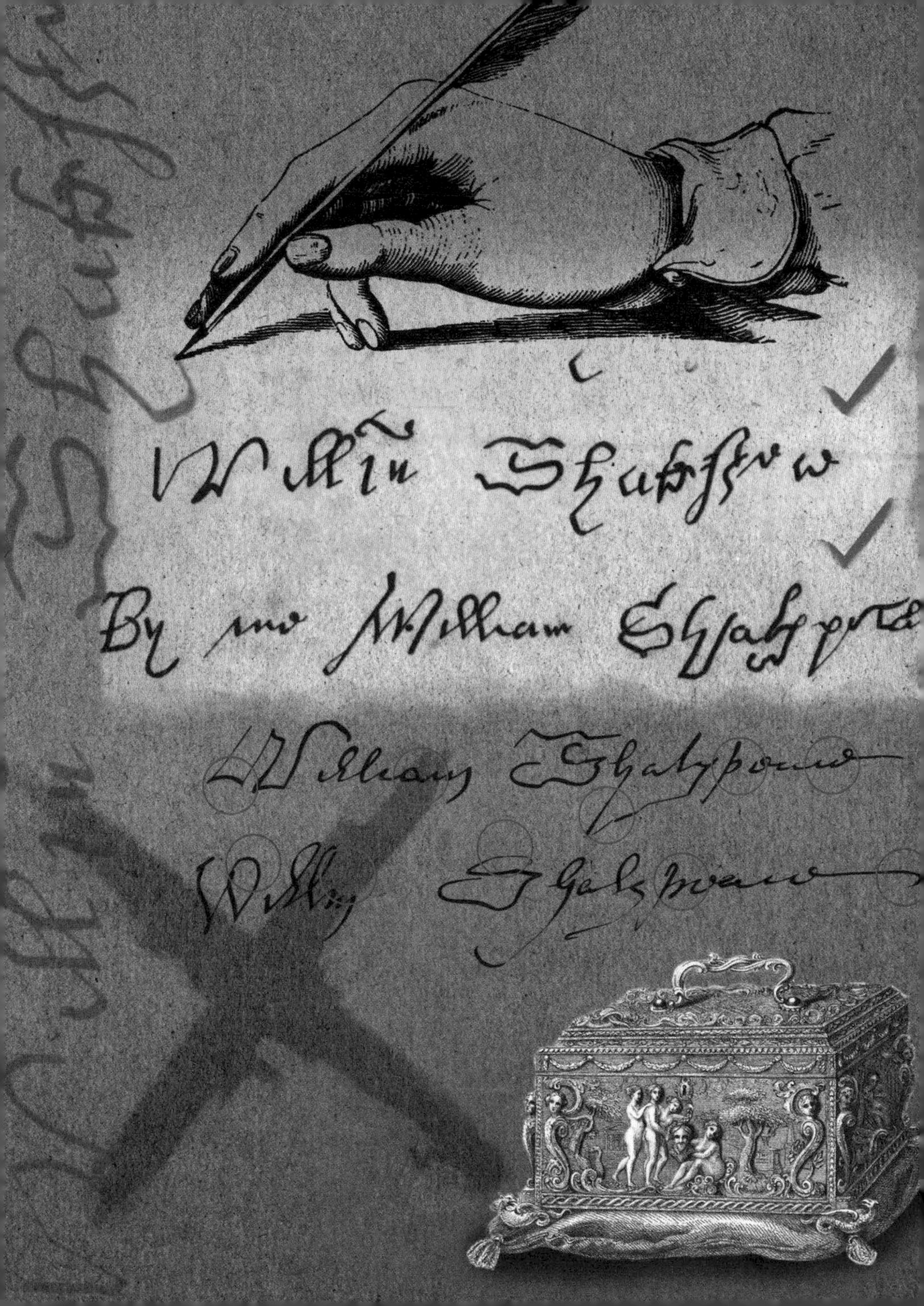

CRITICAL HERITAGE

the 30-second play

3-SECOND PROMPT
In his 400-year journey from a mortal to a god, Shakespeare's genius has seemingly never been equalled. Why is that?

3-MINUTE CALL
To what extent is Shakespeare's reputation due to the publication, in 1623, of the *First Folio*? In the preface, Ben Jonson calls him 'star of poets' and 'soul of the age!' saying he is 'for all time'. Eighteen of *The Folio*'s 36 plays were not previously published and otherwise might have been lost. No one knows who funded – or gathered the materials for – this substantial volume, but we owe them a debt of thanks.

Though he was acknowledged as a great writer in his own era, it was not until the 18th century that Shakespeare began to emerge as the pre-eminent writer in English. The well-respected Samuel Johnson, author of the first comprehensive dictionary of the English language, declared in a preface to an edition of his works in 1765 'Shakespeare is above all writers... the poet that holds up to his readers a faithful mirror of manners and of life.' At the end of the century, Samuel Taylor Coleridge's influential lectures and essays raised the status of *Hamlet*, which previously had been mocked and belittled. The Bardolatry that began in the 18th century became something of a national religion in the 19th and claims for Shakespeare have been enlarging ever since: in 2011, the American critic Harold Bloom declared 'Shakespeare is God'. The man himself remains a mystery; we have no knowledge of the personal qualities and life circumstances that forged him, and in turn, forged so many aspects – and the dominant language – of Western culture. Is the mystery part of his durability? Fay Weldon has said that if she found Shakespeare's diary, she'd burn it. In 400 years, Shakespeare has become the writer of whom everyone has heard, but nobody knows. 'My name be buried where my body is'? Hardly.

RELATED TOPICS
See also
THE LIFE & LEGEND
page 16

INFLUENCE
page 144

APOCRYPHA
page 148

FORGERIES
page 150

3-SECOND BIOGRAPHIES
BEN JONSON
1572–1637
Poet, playwright and literary critic

SAMUEL JOHNSON
1709–1784
Literary critic, editor, biographer and essayist

HAROLD BLOOM
1930–
Literary critic

30-SECOND TEXT
Ros Barber

William Shakespeare is now so revered that he is like a literary god.

RESOURCES

BOOKS

Dating Shakespeare's Plays:
A Critical Review of the Evidence
Kevin Gilvary
(Parapress, 2010)

English Renaissance Drama
Peter Womack
(Blackwell, 2006)

The First Two Quartos of Hamlet:
A New View of the Origins and
Relationship of the Texts
Margrethe Jolly
(McFarland, 2014)

Shakespeare: The World as a Stage
Bill Bryson
(HarperCollins, 2007)

Shakespeare, Co-Author: A Historical
Study of Five Collaborative Plays
Brian Vickers
(Oxford University Press, 2004)

Shakespeare as Literary Dramatist
Lukas Erne
(Cambridge University Press, 2005)

The Shakespearean Stage 1574–1642
Andrew Gurr
(Cambridge University Press, 1992)

Shakespeare's Sonnets
Katherine Duncan-Jones
(Arden Shakespeare, 1997)

Shakespeare's Unorthodox Biography:
New Evidence of an Authorship Problem
Diana Price
(Greenwood Press, 2000)

The Truth about William Shakespeare:
Fact, Fiction and Modern Biographies
David Ellis
(Edinburgh University Press, 2012)

Ungentle Shakespeare:
Scenes from His Life
Katherine Duncan-Jones
(Arden Shakespeare, 2001)

Who Wrote Shakespeare?
John Michell
(Thames & Hudson Ltd, 1996)

Will In the World: How Shakespeare
Became Shakespeare
Stephen Greenblatt
(Bodley Head, 2014)

William Shakespeare: A Documentary Life
Samuel Schoenbaum
(Oxford University Press, 1975)

WEBSITES

deep.sas.upenn.edu
Database of early English playbooks.

doubtaboutwill.org
Website of The Shakespeare Authorship
Coalition, dedicated to raising awareness
of doubts about the identity of William
Shakespeare.

firstfolio.bodleian.ox.ac.uk
The *First Folio* online.

folger.edu
Website of the Folger Shakespeare
Library.

luminarium.org
A useful resource for Renaissance
English literature.

mapoflondon.uvic.ca
Map of early modern London.

opensourceshakespeare.org
rhymezone.com/shakespeare
The complete works of
Shakespeare online (searchable).

quartos.org
The Shakespeare Quartos Archive.

shakespeareauthorship.com
Website dedicated to the proposition
that Shakespeare wrote Shakespeare.

shakespeare-online.com
shakespeares-sonnets.com
Online study guides to Shakespeare's
plays and sonnets.

NOTES ON CONTRIBUTORS

EDITOR

Ros Barber is a lecturer in Creative and Life Writing at Goldsmiths College, University of London, a Visiting Research Fellow at the University of Sussex, and Director of Research at the Shakespearean Authorship Trust. Her articles on Shakespeare, and on his contemporary Christopher Marlowe, have been published in both academic journals and more mainstream outlets. She is author of the verse novel *The Marlowe Papers*, published by Sceptre (2012) in the UK and St Martin's Press (2013) in the US, and written entirely in Shakespearean blank verse.

FOREWORD

Mark Rylance is an actor. He was for ten years the Artistic Director of Shakespeare's Globe theatre. He is a trustee of the Shakespearean Authorship Trust and an Honorary Bencher of The Middle Temple Hall. He wrote a play, *I am Shakespeare*.

CONTRIBUTORS

Jessica Dyson is a lecturer in English Literature at the University of Portsmouth, specializing in Early Modern Drama. Her published research discusses the representation of law and authority in commercial theatre drama under Charles I. Her current research explores the changing relationship between madness and justice played out on the early modern stage.

Andrew James Hartley (Robinson Professor of Shakespeare Studies, University of North Carolina, Charlotte) is a performance scholar and theatre practitioner. His published work on Shakespeare includes books on dramaturgy, the performance history of *Julius Caesar*, political theatre, and university stagings. As A. J. Hartley (www.ajhartley.net) he is also a best-selling novelist.

Margrethe Jolly is a college lecturer in English Literature and Language turned independent researcher. She is author of *The First Two Quartos of Hamlet*, investigating which *Hamlet* quarto was written first.

Claire van Kampen was Associate Artistic Director of Shakespeare's Globe theatre in London from its opening in 1997, and Founding Director of Theatre Music. She has created music for more than 50 of the Globe's productions, as well as composing for film and TV, including the BBC's *Wolf Hall* (2015). She has continued to be the Globe Associate for Early Modern Music since 2007, and lectures on historical music for the Globe faculty as well as continuing to create music there and for other theatre productions (both Shakespeare and otherwise) on Broadway and in London's West End.

Kirk Melnikoff is an Associate Professor in the Department of English at the University of North Carolina, Charlotte. He has edited two collections – *Writing Robert Greene* (Ashgate, 2008) and *Robert Greene* (Ashgate, 2011) – and his critical work has appeared in many journals and essay collections. He is currently editing *Edward II: A Critical Reader for Arden* and is finishing a monograph entitled *Elizabethan Book Trade Publishing and the Endeavors of Literary Culture*.

Lynn Robson is a lecturer in early modern literature at Regent's Park College, University of Oxford. She has published articles on popular murder stories from the 16th and 17th centuries and is currently working on the significance of kneeling in Shakespeare's plays.

Lee Joseph Rooney is a doctoral candidate at the University of Liverpool whose thesis is on prophecy in Shakespeare's English history plays.

Earl Showerman is a retired physician and independent scholar who has published a series of peer-reviewed articles on Shakespeare's use of Greek dramatic sources in *Hamlet*, *Macbeth*, *Timon of Athens*, *The Winter's Tale*, *Much Ado About Nothing* and *A Midsummer Night's Dream*. His article, 'How Did Shakespeare Learn the Art of Medicine?' was included in a recent collection of essays, *Shakespeare Beyond Doubt?* He currently teaches Shakespeare studies at the Osher Lifelong Learning Institute of Southern Oregon University.

Robin Williams received her doctorate from Brunel University, London and is focused on organizing a return to the tradition of reading Shakespeare out loud and in community. She publishes *The Shakespeare Papers* bimonthly and is developing a line of Shakespeare plays edited and designed specifically for adult reading groups.

INDEX

ACKNOWLEDGEMENTS

PICTURE CREDITS

The publisher would like to thank the following individuals and organizations for their kind permission to reproduce the images in this book. Every effort has been made to acknowledge the pictures; however, we apologize if there are any unintentional omissions.

Fotolia: 61L.
Getty Images: /Heritage Images: 72L; /Hulton Archive /Stringer: 31 (fourth from left).
iStock: 11, 133T, 27TR, 31 (third & fifth from left), 33BL&BR, 58R, 73R.
Library of Congress Prints and Photographs Division Washington, D.C.: 47L, 49BR, 123C, 143 background, 145BL&TC.
Rex Features: Moviestore Collection/REX: 143 C&R.
Shutterstock, Inc./www.shutterstock.com: Front cover, 2, 7, 17B&T, 19 background, 21C, 25L&R, 31T, 31B first & second from left, 39R, 41 main image & background, 47C, 53 background, 61R, 67T, 69B, 69T, 81 background, 83BL, 83TL, 85T&BR, 93B & background, 119T & background, 139B, 141, 145BC, 153.
Thinkstock: 19L&R, 39L.
Wellcome Library London: 131 main image & BC.

AUTHOR ACKNOWLEDGEMENTS

I would like to thank Caroline Earle and Jacqui Sayers at Ivy Press for asking me to create this book, and for their unstinting support and patience as I did so. A debt of gratitude is owed to Bill Leahy, who recommended me as editor, for Jane Roe, who patiently copy-edited the text, and Tom Kitch, who covered the business end. Most importantly I would like to thank all the contributors for their timely and apposite contributions – it is no mean feat to boil down to 300 words subjects on which whole books have been written – and for their tolerant incorporation of my editorial suggestions. We hold it true that 'joy's soul lies in the doing'.